*the gift of the game*

*also by* **TOM ALLEN**

Toe Rubber Blues: Mid-Life Thoughts on the Prospects of Aging

Rolling Home: A Cross-Canada Railroad Memoir

*a* **FATHER,** *a* **SON,** *and the* **WISDOM** *of* **HOCKEY**

**ANCHOR CANADA**

# the
# GIFT
## of the
# GAME

**TOM ALLEN**

Library and Archives Canada Cataloguing in Publication

Allen, Tom, 1961–
The gift of the game : a father, a son, and the wisdom of
hockey / Tom Allen.

ISBN-13: 978-0-385-66079-2
ISBN-10: 0-385-66079-0

1. Allen, Tom, 1961-. 2. Hockey. 3. Fathers and sons. I. Title.

PS8551.L55572Z467 2006    796.962    C2006-902687-4


Cover image: Loretta Ray / Getty Images
Cover design: CS Richardson
Printed and bound in Canada

Published in Canada by
Anchor Canada, a division of
Random House of Canada Limited

Visit Random House of Canada Limited's website:
www.randomhouse.ca

TRANS    10    9    8    7    6    5    4    3    2    1

*For Wesley,*
*for Melissa*
*and for Lori*

# CONTENTS

## THANKS

Melissa Allen
Pauline Allen
Philip Allen
Wesley Allen
Rob Anthony
Peter Clark
Greig Clarke
Jan Cornish
Doug Crozier
Al Franklin
Mark Franklin
Peter Gemmell
Johh Gotziaman
Michael Harvey
Mark Kelley
John Kimmel

Roman Kowalczyszyn
Adam Laufer
Ganesh Mohan
Dave Picton
Paul Scott
Peter Shier
Ian Trickett
Dave Trombley
Bernie Walczak
Ted Weber
Heather White

As I was finishing this book, Jerry Johnson, a mentor to me, died of leukemia at fifty-five years old. He remains an enormous influence.

A special thanks to my editor, Martha Kanya-Forstner, and to Scott Sellers, both of Doubleday. Scott suggested the idea, suggested interesting people to talk to and even came up with the title. If his side hadn't won in the 2004 PEN Canada Writers vs. Publishers game, Scott would be perfect.

Lori Gemmell has listened to every word of this book, and thousands more. She is an inspiration and a joy and I cannot thank her enough.

The Leaside Flames atom, minor pee wee and pee wee select teams, 2002–2004: Wesley Allen, Evan Blair, James Bolt, Devlin Brand, Charlie Casper, Chris Fallis, Jonathan Hart, Sam Hildebrand, Matti Keskikyla, Andrew Kowalczyszyn, Harrison Levy, Ryan Malion,

Taylor Martin, Patrick Maulson, Devin Montrose, Derek Perry, Shawn Phyper, Reed Picton, Nathan Robbins-Kanter, Ben Sankey, Matthew Silverstein, Alex Small, Aidan Totten and Robert Zend-Gabori.

The Vultures, 2003–2005: Dave "Army" Allaway, Bruce Bullock, Andre Cleghorn, Steve Easton, Kevin Ely, Val Gigante, Cliff Good, Dave Gort, Blair Hogg, Daryl Jackson, Dave Kinnear, Chris Maxwell, Joseph McLuckie, Jonathan Mingay, Mike Muise, Les Nip, Don Pecora, Guy Perry, Brock Smith, Cam "Bubbles" Stewart, Terece Tai, Noel Thomas and Eric "Woody" Van Wolde.

The Gill family Saturday-night shinny game: Philip Bauer, Debbie Burke, Alicia Butler, Michael Charbonneau, Pat and Gord Deane, Marielle DeBleser, April Dequanne, Lori Dermott, Michele Dunsford, Heather, Jeff and Kevin Gill, Heather Lawrie, Michelle Lecce, Sue Lister, Karen and Jim Marlow, Mike Martino, Denise and John McLean, Nancy and Greg McLeod, Danny Meneses, Al Nault, Justin Parker, Janice Pietrantonio, Mia Poscente, Scott Reiner, Scott Sellers, Winston Sue-Wah-Sing, Nori Takahashi, Joe Tanti and Todd Timmerman.

Philip and Pauline Allen

Lac Croche, 2001

# INTRODUCTION

I CAN TELL YOU EXACTLY when and where it started: March 2001, on Lac Croche, near Saint-Donat, in the Laurentians in Quebec. My parents live on the shore of Lac Croche. We were there to visit and ski for March break.

Normally, Lac Croche is buried in snow by March. It's common practice to shovel off the roof in mid-winter, leaving a pile of snow so big it will take you right onto the top of the house, as if you were going upstairs. Snow forts are great fun. There is a network of snowmobile trails throughout the area, good cross-country skiing and some of the most developed ski areas in the country.

Skating, though, can be tricky.

First of all, Lac Croche isn't really a lake at all. It's a loopy detour in the Ouareau River, and there are currents that shift the ice, making slushy patches that won't usually give out completely, but will soak you from the knees down. The same snow that is a blessing for every other winter activity makes a decent rink almost impossible. Most years it starts accumulating before the lake has really frozen and insulates the slushy mess below, keeping it that way all winter. If, by chance, there is good ice at the start of the season, shovelling it can take an hour or two per day, and even then the ice ends up pitted, flaky and riddled with cracks that will swallow a skate blade whole and give the skater above a very nasty surprise. Most of the time, bringing skates to Lac Croche indicated unrealistic expectations at best.

Unrealistic expectations were not at all out of character for me at the time. I was in the eleventh year of a marriage that had barely survived on a mixed diet of determination, denial and fevered dependence on whatever good times happened along. I counted on March break at Lac Croche to be one of those times. The place held wonderful childhood memories for me, and between days spent in winter beauty and evenings spent with warm, homemade meals in a loving, stable home, I allowed myself to feel I was providing my children some of the luxuries I'd grown up with myself.

The winter of 2001 was an El Niño winter. January and February saw several thaws, and by March, instead of mountains of snow, there was a rotting grey carpet on the forest floor with cruddy spots of gravel and leaves poking through. It rained all day Tuesday, and the temperature dropped to minus-30 that night. The cross-country trails were treacherous, the ski hills were bulletproof, and even a walk through the woods became a trial: the crust on the snow wouldn't hold you up, but with each step you would mangle your shins. March break wasn't looking dependable at all.

The lake ice, though, was spectacular. The sky was clear and blue on Wednesday morning, and the frozen lake was glassy and smooth from one side clear across to the other, with only faint ridges where snowmobile tracks had been, and not a speck of snow.

It was a good thing we'd decided to bring the skates. Melissa, who was six, was still somewhat tentative about it, but when she did skate, she did it with the same steady determination that she'd bring to most tasks. If she got what she felt was too much encouragement, or if what we called encouragement had become something more like parental pressure, she'd go inside.

Eight-year-old Wesley was somewhat keener. We'd started him skating when he was three, and he cried most the time. It wasn't much fun. But on his fourth birthday, in December of the next winter, he figured it out. I took him to the gate at the outdoor public rink. He held the boards for a second, pushed off and skated a full lap, his eyes full of wonder. "I can skate now," he said. "Because I'm four."

We signed him up for a power skating and hockey program that winter. It wasn't entirely successful. Sometimes he was discouraged. Sometimes he said everyone else was better than him. Sometimes all he wanted to do was go home. Like a few other dads, I started going out on the ice, too, to try and boost his confidence, and that's how, in my mind, hockey became a game that Wesley played with my help.

In his second year I signed on as an assistant coach of his house-league team. The year after that the games were at 6:30, Saturday mornings. Wesley and I are both morning people. I'd wake him up at 5:30, feed him, get to the arena as soon as it opened at 5:55, help him dress, lace up his skates and join him on the ice for twenty minutes till the game started. We'd pass and shoot, or play one on one. Sometimes we'd just hack around and bash into each other. I looked forward to it all week.

I'd become a Hockey Dad, thereby perpetrating one of the greatest frauds in Canadian hockey history. I knew nothing—really nothing—about coaching or playing organized hockey.

I grew up in Montreal, on the heels of the great Maurice Richard–era Canadiens dynasty and at the beginning of the Scotty Bowman squads of the '70s. That, however, didn't help my game a whole lot. I played one season of house-league hockey at Montreal West Arena in 1969, when I was eight. I'd grown two inches the previous summer and my ankles were like rubber. I was a sensitive child who tended to cry a lot. The kid next door told me I was weak, and I believed him. I think I spent quite a lot of time on the bench, but I'm not sure even about that. The only memory I have of the entire season is of standing alone on my ankles in my own end, my feet splayed out, hoping the play would stay on the other side of the rink.

I said I didn't like hockey. My parents were relieved to have their Saturdays back, and the next winter they signed us all up for ski lessons. That was that.

I still owned skates, though, and sometimes I goofed around on the outdoor rink, but not very often. For an anglophone Montrealer in the 1970s, playing hockey turned out to be like speaking French. Everyone assumed you could, but you didn't really need to.

So, I went to public skating at the arena on Friday nights with my gang of friends, and didn't notice that because we always went counter-clockwise, I never learned to turn right. I played hours of ball hockey on the driveway, imagining myself outhustling, outshooting and flat-out flattening the current stars of the game, never noticing that banging a tennis ball into the net wasn't teaching me how to shoot. I watched hours of hockey on TV, not noticing that watching the Habs win year after year hadn't taught me anything at all about how the game was won.

Then, thirty years later, I found myself stepping into a postcard image sent directly from the Postmaster General of Canadian Mythology: on shining Lac Croche, on an incredible blue-sky mid-March morning, playing hockey with my eight-year-old son.

We'd been out on the lake for about an hour. At first we skated everywhere, just because we could, but then we dragged chunks of firewood out to the middle of the lake for goalposts and played a game.

Competition between a parent and child is a matter of balance, and it shifts from year to year, as the child grows and develops and the parent matures and decays. We both enjoyed playing together, and most of the time I would make sure he won, but neither of us would have any fun if that was too obvious, and if I was winning by too much the whole thing could fall apart into tears, accusations, guilt, frustration and something very far from what I'd pictured when we started out.

We were headed that way again that morning. I was up by two goals, and because our game was getting faster and faster, artfully failing was beginning to require more skill than I possessed. Then Wes came into my zone from the right wing, faked to the outside, slid the puck between my legs, skated around me, picked up the puck again and scored. We both cheered. It was a nice move and he had legitimately beaten me.

Then he did it again.

And again.

I couldn't stop him. If I tried going for the puck, he'd pull it away. If I blocked the gap between my skates, he'd just go around me.

He scored five times like that.

I said it was about time we went inside.

I was proud of him, and I didn't feel too badly about my own play. I had never pretended to be a hockey player, and to see the way Wesley was moving and handling the puck, and feeling so good about what he'd learned to do, I couldn't help but think that at least one of us, and maybe both, were successes.

Wesley's house-league team won the championship

that year. That win, and perhaps the memory of so thoroughly deking out his old man, seemed to give him a bit of a push. He started practising more, and I decided that from then on I'd leave the coaching to people who actually knew the game.

That fall, Wesley announced he was going to try out for the "select" team—a kind of house-league all-star squad. Anyone can play house-league hockey, if they have equipment and have paid the registration fee. The higher levels—"select," "A," "AA" and so on—all require a tryout, and the competition is usually very tight. Select tryouts might see five players vying for each spot on the team. At the higher levels it can be three or four times that.

The select coaches had scheduled a series of skating and stickhandling sessions that were open to all house-league players and were billed as a chance to get warmed up for the season. After that, there were three tryouts, with cuts after each. The practice sessions were held at the beginning of the school year, usually at dinnertime, at a rink at the other end of a highway that was routinely clogged for most of the evening. I have since learned that, because of competition for ice, such inconvenience is built right into the culture of hockey in this country. At the time, however, it seemed monstrous arrogance to me, and a sign that hockey was a sport a healthy family might choose to keep at a distance. We skipped the drill sessions. If hockey was going to take over the house, I figured, there was no point in helping it.

The select team took fifteen players that year; Wesley was the sixteenth. We were both left wondering what might have happened if I'd taken him to those extra skating sessions, but it was too late. The night the coach called to tell him he'd been cut, I went to check on him when he was in bed and I saw a picture of sadness that I will never forget.

Wesley had a great season in house league that year. Most games he was a dominant player, sometimes better than the select players who'd beaten him for a spot on the team, but that wasn't enough. He never stopped waiting for the call. If the select coach turned up in the stands at a game, Wesley would notice, and would look up after every poke check, every rush, every pass, every goal. After his best games he'd change extra slowly, giving that coach time to stumble upon him in the dressing room and suddenly be struck by the error in his ways.

It never happened.

So, Wesley played every chance he got. He played shinny every week on the outdoor rink. He took part in a bunch of shoestring outdoor tournaments around the city. He made the public school team and went with them to the city championship—in the Air Canada Centre, no less—and spent just about every spare moment he could find on skates.

The next season, the select team that had cut him moved up and became an "A" team, but he didn't bother trying out for that squad this time. There was plenty of room on what became the new select team, and that was what he wanted.

Wesley was thrilled when he made it, and so was I, but the reality was that while Wesley would be getting more ice time than he'd ever had, I would be spending the next eight months driving him to one or two practices and two games per week. As well as tournaments throughout the season, I could also look forward to hellish rush-hour drives to games on the other side of the city that started when people should have been enjoying seconds at dinner. And about a thousand dollars in fees.

That wasn't all. I was getting seconds when I got a call from Roman, the assistant coach, whose son Andrew was also on the team.

They needed another coach.

If it had happened a year earlier, I might have declined, but things had changed. After staggering on for another year and a half, the marriage that had brought Wesley and Melissa into the world was lurching through its final steps. I had hopes for what might happen to my life with my children once their mother and I parted, but they were only hopes. Nothing was certain, and here, for the price of pretending once again that I understood the game of hockey, was a guarantee of seeing Wesley at least twice a week, and maybe even a few extra hours with just the two of us. Sure, those hours would be in the car, in rush-hour traffic, but my standards had changed. It was a chance to be part of the activity he loved most, and, maybe, a chance to extend the fantasy that hockey, this game he'd discovered he could play so well, was still something he did with my help. I warned Roman—and Dave, the head coach—that they were getting someone whose meagre administrative skills still far outweighed his value on the ice. They said that was fine.

About a month later, I moved to an apartment around the corner, and my relationship to hockey changed radically. Even though I'd avoided it both as a child and an adult, this game that grips our nation had managed to get a stranglehold on me. Like so many others in Canada, I was now using the hockey rink as a workshop to repair the shattered connection between myself and my son, and to work out my own value as a man and a father.

I was a lousy hockey player, and had been one for all of my forty-one years. Then, in one swipe, the drive to skate, shoot and pass gripped me as if my very worth depended on it—which, irrationally or not, it did. There were entire winter days when I was on my own, and skating turned out to be one of the few things that actually got me through the afternoon.

And hockey turned out to be fun. Beginning to feel some strength in my stride coming out of a wrong-side turn (that is, a clockwise turn, the turn I'd neglected at the arena on Friday nights as a kid) was exhilarating. Hanging onto the puck while slaloming through a set of pylons felt fantastic. Skating backwards felt fantastic. And, just as it had been when I was a kid in the driveway, a lot of the joy of playing hockey was inside my head. The difference was,

THE GIFT OF THE GAME

instead of imagining myself as Jean Beliveau streaking across centre ice, I imagined myself as myself, but better: the dad who could skate, the dad who could land the puck right on the tape of his son's stick and then trail behind, waiting for the rebound that never came because that brilliant son faked left, swooped right and drilled a wrist shot into the top corner, then turned, his arms raised as he jumped into his dad's arms in celebration.

That fantasy felt like a connection between us. If I could make that happen, perhaps my son and I would have something no crisis could shake for the rest of our lives.

But the truth was, I didn't know that. I didn't know if hockey could do that, or anything else, or even if I had it in me to learn to really play at all. About all I *did* know was that I had lots of time on my own, and what felt like very little to lose.

2002–2003

Courtesy Janitis Photography

**LEASIDE 2002–03 ATOM SELECT FLAMES**
*Front:* Patrick Maulson, Ben Sankey, Sam Hildebrand, Shawn
Phyper, Derek Perry, Nathan Robbins-Kanter, Chris Fallis,
Charlie Casper, Matti Keskikyla.
*Middle:* Reed Picton, Wesley Allen, Devlin Brand, Taylor Martin,
James Bolt, Matthew Silverstein, Andrew Kowalczyszyn.
*Back:* Me, Dave Picton, Roman Kowalczyszyn, Anne Phyper
*Missing:* Alex Small.

I

I AM SPRAWLED ON MY SIDE in the corner of a hockey rink, wondering what happened. There are twenty people staring at me. One of them is my son, Wesley.

Wesley and I are both here because we have a position on this year's Leaside Flames select hockey team for the atom age group. Wesley is a player; I'm an assistant coach. The head coach is Dave Picton. The other assistant coach is Roman Kowalczyszyn, whose name is a lot easier to say than you might think, but most of us still call him Roman.

Dave has been working on positioning in our own end. The players are learning to adjust their positions as the puck moves around the zone. Dave asked for a coach to play the part of the puck, and I volunteered. I skated hard towards the corner. Then, with about six feet to go, I caught an edge and flew, just as many other pucks do, right into the boards.

"Are you okay?" Dave asks. The rest are silent.

I am okay. I think my shoulder took the brunt of the blow.

"Fine. Yeah," I say, forcing a laugh as I get up. "Caught an edge."

Until now I have only played the role of barking encourager ("Come on! That's it! Dig! Dig!") and puck farmer. There are thirty to forty pucks on the ice during most practices, and if they have to be moved from one place to another, I'm your man.

But fast, graceful skating, ease going both forwards and backwards, accelerating crossover turns, artful stick-handling, sizzling shots to the top corner, cool-under-pressure tape-to-tape passes to the man in front of the net, and even a time-deepened understanding of the game are all well beyond my abilities. Most days I am conscious that I am getting more from this arrangement than the team is.

There is no secret about this. I am an assistant coach because Dave and Roman needed another person to help out, and I said I would do what I could.

Dave and Roman are both very good skaters. Dave has long legs, and when he pushes off he uses all of that length and power. His quick laps after practice are an inspiring sight.

Roman also skates beautifully, and he has a slap shot like a cannon. He grew up in a little town outside of Thunder Bay, Ontario, where there were three things to do on a Saturday night: play hockey, watch hockey or go curling. You played hockey when you were young, you watched hockey when your kids were playing, and you curled after that. If you were really old, you watched curling.

Dave and Roman are good-natured men. I am certain their tolerance for my lack of hockey ability and experience will one day wear thin, but for now I feel that, even as a barking puck farmer, I have a reason to be here.

"Here," by the way, is a dingy arena at the edge of a business park on the northern border of Toronto. It is called New Centre Ice, but it has been a while since it was what you would call new, and it certainly isn't at the centre of anything. There are two full artificial rinks, small dressing rooms, eternally leaking showers and a pro shop that is usually closed—all built into a strip mall with a Chinese buffet, a few nondescript import businesses and a bar that has been trying to open under new management for two years. The grey lobby has three or four video games whose soundtracks blare screams and gunshots day and night. If you should find yourself at New Centre Ice with time to spare, and are not tempted by any of the above-listed charms, you would be well advised to make sure you have the use of a car. A half-hour's walk in any direction yields warehouses, parking lots, sealed office complexes and one restaurant, a very long way to the south, that used to be a Pizza Hut but isn't anymore.

This is where my son and I, his teammates, my fellow

coaches and a few parents will spend ninety minutes of our Saturday mornings from now until April. It is, as much as any place, our hockey home. I can already make the trip here without thinking about it.

• • •

Most of the players on the team live in Leaside, a tony neighbourhood of brick homes and stately maples just above the northern edge of what people think of as downtown Toronto. It is a comfortable little neighbourhood that can be divided into a good side and a better one. The big-box grocery store in Leaside stocks high-end gas barbeques as an impulse item.

I live in the less stately Riverdale, an adjacent area populated by left-leaning professionals, media personalities, retired rock stars, actors and symphony musicians. The main artery, Danforth Avenue, offers a critical mass of Greek restaurants, alternative health practitioners and a store that leads the nation in the sale of tofurkey, a turkey-shaped chunk of fermented bean curd that allows the conscientious Thanksgiving or Christmas cook to avoid killing anything.

My home is a few blocks from the Danforth. It is a one-bedroom apartment on the second floor of a three-storey brick house that has been converted into flats. The building is also home to a woman and her two-year-old daughter and two male actors. And, as of this week, two afternoons and one night per week, it is home to my children: Wesley, ten years old, and his sister, Melissa, who is eight. Their other home is with their mother, around the corner and down the street.

I moved here on an early-November Sunday evening in 2002, after what so far counts as the most difficult moment in my life: a conversation at the kitchen table with my children, in which I spoke words that had been echoing in my head for several years but that I still hoped never to say.

"Your mother and I are separating," I told them. "I am moving to an apartment around the corner. I'm leaving tonight."

I have almost no detailed memory of the next few hours. I told them where I'd be living, and we walked there together. They saw the empty rooms, the old fridge, light streaming in from the streetlamp onto the hardwood floor, and we walked back, numb. Their mother took them out to a restaurant so they wouldn't have to witness anything else that night. After they had stepped out the door, I stood in the front hall for a few seconds, staring at nothing. The rest is a blur.

I brought a table, three chairs, a futon, a dresser, a pile of artwork that had been in boxes in the basement and heaps of clothes, all dragged out at a steady, manic pace. I couldn't stop moving—unpacking pictures, setting up the bed, assembling the table, putting away clothes, sweating as I went, until the pictures were lined up along the kitchen walls, the dresser was full beside the futon, and the phone sat in the middle of the empty living room, in front of the bare picture window, its cord snaking back across the floor to the outlet in the wall.

I remember lying down on the futon, on my stomach, eyes open, staring at the baseboard on the wall in front of me, waiting for sleep.

Over the next few days, friends astonished me. Ted gave me a sofa and an armchair. Mark donated an old television. Peter gave an amplifier, Bernie speakers, and John a CD player. Music, TV and something to sit on. Guys, right? What else *would* I need? I went to Ikea for shelves, to the dollar store for a frying pan and to Canadian Tire for a toaster. After years as a gainfully employed member of mainstream society, the only things that were now truly mine were the things I'd started out with after school: ski equipment, old records, camping gear, a Frisbee, a few clothes and a bass trombone. It was as if I'd highlighted all of my worldly possessions—house, carpets, furniture, china, silver, the objects our society considers the material evidence of maturity—and pressed "delete."

In keeping with this suddenly collegiate life, I did what I would have done back then at a time of crisis—I went home to Mom and Dad.

My parents had been more than generous in preserving the bits of my childhood. I hadn't lived under their roof for twenty-two years, but stashed in the garage next to their house in the Laurentian mountains, north of Montreal, were the desk and dresser I'd had in my bedroom as a child and the bunk beds my father built for me when I was eight.

I knew that nothing my parents could say would change my situation. I knew that many people my age no longer have parents to run home to. I knew that this was a time not to be an overgrown child, but to be courageous and to model a strong and independent life for my children, to show them that it was possible to live through—and even grow through—this madness. Something in me, though, believed all of that would be much easier with those bunk beds. They'd been a safe place for me when I was still scared of the dark. I wouldn't be able to give my children stability, at least not for a while, but I wanted them to be able to feel safe at night.

My friend John Kimmel, the one who gave me the CD player, also loaned me his panel van. John's a florist, and he's heard all the jokes, so he drives a big, dark green bad-assed Dodge named Bertha. She's got tinted windows, a menacing grill and suspension as hard as concrete. It's the kind of vehicle that, if you were a cop, you'd think twice before approaching.

Bertha and I blasted down the 401 from Toronto to Montreal, then followed the outlying highways north, through an entire day of unrelenting rain. I can still picture my white knuckles clamped onto the steering wheel as Bertha and I rolled to a stop a full eight hours later.

My parents were waiting. The beds, desk and dresser were in the garage, along with a Bertha-load from my mother: rugs, a vacuum cleaner, towels, kitchen stuff—hand-me-downs she might have thrown out, but kept.

I was back on the road after breakfast the next morning. It was Remembrance Day, and Bertha, for all her space and character, had only an FM radio for company. My choices were eight hours of veteran testimonia on CBC 1 or eight hours of requia on CBC 2, both interspersed with the same hourly newscast, repeated eight times. The alternative was a stream of constantly shifting, yet constantly identical classic-rock stations, offering commercial breaks for car wash services and hydroponic home-grow equipment and repeated exhortations to "Keep on rocking for the vets in the Free World."

I spent the day in silence. When I finally pulled up in front of the apartment in Toronto there was nothing for it but to drag everything up the stairs, assemble the beds, put the clothes in the dresser and the phone on the desk and, again, lie down, heart pounding, stare at the baseboards, and wait for sleep.

• • •

The next morning, I filled a page with names of people to phone, to explain what had happened in my life. It was a grim task, but an important one. I was taking control of my situation. At the top of the list were family, closest friends and, oddly enough, Roman and Dave.

Some people might have called their priest, minister or rabbi. I called my son's hockey coaches.

The conversations were strange. The collapse of a marriage is a deeply intimate matter, and these men weren't intimate friends, but I needed to tell them, if only to let them know that one of their players, my son, was going to be going through a very hard time for the next while. Dave reassured me that he would keep an eye on Wesley and try to support him, which is, I guess, the best I could have hoped for. With Roman it was more difficult; we've known each other since our sons were in the same toddler play group, so this was an event in a life that was, in some ways, parallel to his.

Roman's a very good and honest man, and somehow his response has stayed with me. He tried to offer understanding, and solace, but realized he didn't know enough to be able to do even that. "I'm sorry, Tom," he finally said in a frank but respectful way. "I really don't know what to say."

A few days earlier, I had been part of my children's lives without even trying: hurried meals, negotiations over bedtimes, throwaway conversations about the day (Q: How was school? A: Good.). I was with them all the time—even when I *wasn't*—and never had to question my role in their lives. Now those moments, and especially those everyday moments, were precious and rare, and frighteningly fragile. Nothing was settled legally between their mother and me. I had absolutely no reassurance of what the future would bring.

For ten years my sense of myself as a father grew unquestioned into a central part of my identity, and now it is gone. In the rare moments that I can muster the presence of mind to really look at what has happened, part of me questions whether it will ever return, and whether I really am a parent at all anymore.

My children are with me two afternoons and one night per week, but outside of home life I have no official connection to Melissa. I am her father, but my time with her is tightly prescribed, and beyond that the daily realities of my role are alarmingly shallow. She studies dance and sings in a choir, and my part in those activities is to bring her there and bring her home, and possibly watch or listen. The time when we merely exist together has all but disappeared. I will always be her father, but I have no guarantee of what that will really mean.

However, on the hockey rink, away from the uproar of my domestic life, I know I have a role. I am an assistant coach for my son's hockey team—a crappy coach, fine, but still, a coach. As such, even though he is only one of seventeen boys, and even though he is wearing a suit of armour with a cage over his face and a mouthguard packed around his teeth, and even though he may be dealing with levels of shame and anger and confusion that would rattle people three times his age, I will see him two times every week—once at practice, and once at a game. That much I know.

• • •

I struggle to my feet from the corner of the rink at New Centre Ice and skate back to the blue line as the players, the parents, my co-coaches and my son all watch.

An idea begins to form in my mind. It is a fantasy, something I've conjured to nurse my shredded pride, but it is compelling. I begin to picture myself skating well, moving freely, carrying the puck, gliding with grace and confidence. It brings a tingle to my legs. They can almost feel what they would have to do—to lean easily, to feel the blades gripping the ice as I swing into a turn, cradling the puck and pushing off again the other way.

It's a lovely feeling, but right now Dave wants to run the drill again, so for the moment I am not expected to do any of that. Right now my only responsibility is to be a puck—a less self-destructive one, if possible.

I manage that much—tentatively, but without further incident—and, misty dreams notwithstanding, I am relieved when the Zamboni guy hits the buzzer and it's time to go. Roman, Dave and I collect the pucks and pylons. I find Wesley in one of the dressing rooms, half-undressed, collecting snow from his skate blades and combining it with any other snow he can scrounge from the others. He and Ben are organizing a snowball raid on the other dressing room in the hope of ambushing the biggest kid on the team, James. But when it comes to artificial-ice snowball fights, James, it turns out, is more than just big; he is a skilled tactician. Wesley has barely finished collecting snow when the door bursts open and there is James, fully armed. Both shots miss, a bystander is caught in the crossfire, and retribution is promised, but the snow's all melted by then, anyway, and all that's left is to head home.

Wesley says there are knots in his laces, and asks me to undo his skates for him.

I am happy to help.

## II

WE'RE IN AN ARENA IN NORTH YORK, in the third period, losing 4–2 against a much better team. The players are trying hard, and still in the game, but some signs of despair are beginning to show.

A select team's level of play can vary from year to year. If a player is strong enough, there is a good chance he will move up a level the next season. Occasionally, an entire team moves up, as the Leaside team in Wesley's age group did after last season. They had been together a few years and won the championship at their level. They moved up to the "A" level this year, making room for the team of players I'm involved with now.

From the outside, this team is just the same as that one. They were the Leaside Flames at the select level, and so are we. We have black jerseys for away games, white for home, and so did they. They had a committed group of parents and a team full of eager kids, and so do we. However, their team full of eager kids was experienced, confident and playing at the top end of the scale and ours is, well, not. Most of our players had never competed beyond the house-league level before this year, and even now, two months into the season, a fair number are still struggling with some basic techniques.

Toronto's select youth hockey teams are organized by an overseeing board called the North York Hockey League. Their system treats the first half of the season as exhibition games to see how teams match up. This year the atom teams will be grouped, based on the results of those first games, into three tiers. Because last year's squad finished at the top of the first tier, we're currently playing the teams that finished near the top, as well.

We've played four other games this season, and we've lost them all, convincingly.

Dave has been very frank with the kids about what they can expect for the first half of the year. He's told them we're thinking about the long term, that even though they're not playing the kinds of games they'll want to tell their grandchildren about, they're learning a great deal. From what I can tell, most of them are fine with that. They are excited to be able to say they are on the select team, even if it is among the least select in the league. It's a tribute to Dave and Roman that, despite our record, the team and the parents are quite optimistic.

I guess I must be, too, even though I come home from most of these games with my jaw wired tight from grinding my teeth for so long at a stretch. I am amazed at my urge to yell and scream during the game, even though I am fully aware of how little I have to contribute.

Dave has taken it all—the tension, the losing, the groans in the dressing room afterwards—in stride, and has turned most of it into positive energy. It's been a good demonstration that coaching a losing team, something I thought even I might be able to do fairly naturally, takes a good deal of understanding and subtlety. Dave has most of that. I'm still working on it.

• • •

Only one year ago, hockey had an entirely different place in our lives. I was just beginning to appreciate how important the game had become to my son, and had no idea how important it would become to me.

The signs were all there, though. Wesley never stopped waiting for the select coach who'd passed him up to change his mind.

He ended up easing the pain of rejection with the obvious cure: more hockey. Toronto has forty-odd artificial outdoor rinks in the downtown area, most in public parks that function as community centres. From December to March the rinks offer public skating time, shinny for various age groups, and several timeslots devoted to organized kids' hockey. Kids sign up, pay a nominal fee and are assigned to one of four house-league teams. There is no experience required. Wesley's age group got two hours of ice time every Tuesday night at Withrow Park. Four teams, two games, one hour each.

Somehow, though, it never quite worked out that way. Most nights, the kids who showed up expecting to play for one team were assigned to another to even things out. There were two coaches who acted as referees; they handed out pinnies in red and in blue and the only time anybody sat down was if they were hurt or needed help tying a skate lace. Some nights there were seven kids on each team, sometimes four, sometimes ten, but everybody skated for at least a full hour, and most nights there were kids who would stay on the ice for two hours, and still longer after that if they could.

Almost every hockey parent talks about how they wish their kids could play a less structured game, away from mind-numbing drills and without adults to interfere and tell them what they are supposed to be learning. Well, that's what this was. The referees made sure no one got hurt, the cold made sure no one stood still, and the kids learned on their own about passing, hogging, deking, forechecking, keeping their heads up and spotting opportunities, and they learned it all from the most even-handed teacher in the history of the game: trial and error.

There really was almost no feedback beyond results. Most parents were too cold to cheer. There really is nothing like the particular kind of dampness that takes hold of the outdoor hockey spectator, especially those watching games after dark. The cold latches onto your bootsoles, climbing upwards from there until it has penetrated the very marrow of your bones and even the most vigorous stamping, clapping, pacing and cursing will not root it out.

"Jesus, it's cold," one parent will say, breathing steam into cupped hands.

"That kid in green's got some wheels, eh? Who's he?"

"That's Ben. How cold is it?"

"Minus-10. They said on the news."

"Feels like minus-20."

"Sure does."

"That your kid?"

"Where?"

"There."

"Oh, yeah. Did he score?"

"Think so."

"Jesus, it's cold."

We would console ourselves with the knowledge that there, in the midst of the largest urban sprawl in the country, we were giving our children what we'd all been told was the true Canadian hockey experience: damp, cold nights; hard, cold air; and the lonely echo of a shot against the boards mingled with kids' voices calling for the puck. To complete that romantic picture, you can add the television commercial moment: the frozen adults murmuring happily as the designated parent returned from the lonely cross-park trek to Tim Hortons with coffee for all.

Even so, most of us were out there again the next Tuesday night, and the next, stamping our feet and cursing the cold. There were nights Wesley was so tired he practically fell asleep at dinner, but he would still be waiting at the door with his hockey bag when it was time to play. If any adult mentioned the cold to any of the players after the game, the kids would look up, bewildered, their hair plastered with sweat, wondering what we were talking about.

The highlight of the outdoor season was a weekend tournament held in mid-February. It was one of a number of tournaments at outdoor rinks across the city, leading up to a city-wide championship to be held in the early spring.

The event was restricted to those playing at no higher than the select level, and that ruled out a couple of the Tuesday-night regulars. So, the team that trekked from Withrow Park to the Giovanni Caboto Skating Rink on that damp February Saturday, although it was billed as an all-star team, was a fairly ragtag bunch. The goalie was a foot taller than anyone else on the ice, one defenceman was a foot shorter, and both had put on skates for the first time that winter. There were two or three forwards who had trouble stopping and for whom a loose puck was something to charge past, flail at hopelessly, or fall on. And there were Wesley, Ben and Derek—three friends whose qualification as "all-stars" at that time rested mostly on their flat refusal to give up.

If this is beginning to sound like a Bad News Bears, lovable-losers-take-home-the-gold kind of story, it won't for much longer. The Withrow Park All-Stars had three games that day, and they won exactly none of them. The morning game was against a midtown squad that was only slightly less ragtag than themselves, and by little more than sheer will our boys managed a tie. Next was a west-end team that won convincingly on the back of their one gallingly excellent player who scored all of the team's goals and treated everyone else, including his own teammates, as pylons.

The last game was against the team that most of us had noticed when they arrived by bus that morning. No other team arrived by bus. No other team had matching jerseys. No other team had a full bench. No other team brought along enough fans to line the rink two rows deep.

The Regent Park All-Stars had played two games before they faced Withrow Park, and they'd won them both, and although none of us knew by exactly how much, it wasn't hard to come up with an estimate. Each of their many goals had brought such a roar from their legions of fans that all of us there that day, whether waiting in the chalet or enjoying a latte at La Paloma, half a block away, registered every one.

There were four of us cheering for Withrow Park.

We had our work cut out for us.

Regent Park went ahead early with a goal by the boy who was the team captain and clearly their star. He was built like a refrigerator and was deceptively fast, but his main quality was a fearsomeness that put him anywhere from just this side of proud to well into nasty. The Withrow All-Stars held him to three goals in the first two periods, and that involved more than one goalmouth scramble and even a loose puck fished away from the open net by one of the ankle-drifting, non-stopping defencemen who just happened to wobble by in time to whack the puck away, milliseconds before it would have crossed the line.

Then, in the third period, our boys showed a glimmer of hope. It was as if by simply going the distance as long as they had, they began to see that, despite the crowds and the uniforms, and the bus, this was no different than playing Tuesday nights in the sweat-soaked cold, and all they had to do was to keep going no matter what.

Things really turned around first with Derek, a little player who was the embodiment of big-hearted determination. He skated with an arm-pumping, head-swinging swagger and seemed to be able to keep the puck through a hurricane.

In the third period Derek poke-checked an over-confident winger and tipped the puck to Ben on the left, who then hit Wesley with a pass that found him wide open. The Regent Park goalie barely stopped him, and the huge Regent crowd went silent.

The Regent Park team clearly hadn't been challenged all day, but they were now back on their heels. With about five minutes to go in the game, Wesley ended up charging in on the goalie, this time all alone, when the tough Regent Park captain caught up with him and hauled him to the ice.

The referee called a penalty shot. Wesley started out at centre, skated in hard with his head down, and put the puck right into the goalie's pads. The Regent crowd went wild, the Withrow boys hung their heads, and twenty seconds later that same Regent captain scored for the fourth time, and that's how the game ended.

I was, I have to admit, a little flushed by the whole thing. I'd been yelling my head off for most of the third period, and now felt an odd mixture of pride, sadness, resentment and a yearning to comfort my son, who'd given, I could tell, all he had and then some.

"Dad!" Wesley said as he came off the ice. "What were you so angry about? We were doing our best, you know. It doesn't help to yell at us."

I was stunned. Even in my most passionate moments I'd stuck with my resolution to only say positive things. I may, it's true, have been *thinking* something like "No, no! Don't pass it *there!* Can't you see?" but I hadn't said those things. Instead I'd said "Skate, skate!" and "Go, Derek, go!" and "Pass! Pass!" or "Shoot!! Shoot!!"

"It sounds like you're yelling," he said, clearly frustrated and embarrassed. "Your voice sounds angry. Why don't you cheer like Guy does?"

Guy is Derek's father. He's a good hockey player, with, not surprisingly, grown-up versions of many of Derek's gifts. He's also a soccer coach who has spent many summers helping kids learn how to play team sports. I took a second or two to wind up my courage. Being sent to ask for cheering lessons seemed like a new low in parenthood. I found Guy in the lobby a few minutes later.

"Um." I hesitated. "Wesley tells me I'm cheering the wrong way and I should do it more like you," I started in, half-expecting to be dismissed as a fool, or worse, a naïve father who actually listened to his frustrated child after a difficult game.

"I try to only say things like 'Well done,'" he said, happy that someone had noticed. "I try to never tell them what to do. I try to wait until they do something good and then encourage them. That way they learn to trust their own instincts and they believe in themselves, instead of me."

It suddenly seemed obvious. It also explained a pattern I'd noticed for years when the boys played house-league soccer. Guy's teams usually started out near the bottom of the pack but almost always hit a winning stride in the fall tournament, as if their understanding of the game had taken longer, but meant more when it came.

I spent a moment absorbing the obviousness of what I'd learned, and then, feeling new respect for my then nine-year-old son, I said "Well done" a few more times than necessary and drove us both home.

• • •

Wesley's involvement in those outdoor games never stopped being valuable. There was a second outdoor tournament later that winter, and a second unstoppable Regent Park team, but even after the rinks were closed for the year, the memory of those frozen Tuesday nights stayed fresh, if for no other reason than it was truly neighbourhood hockey.

Months later, walking on the Danforth in the early-summer sunshine, I would find myself saying hello to kids I somehow recognized, even though I'd only ever seen them with caged faces and steam rising off their sweaty shoulders on those frigid Tuesday nights. Wesley was deeply impressed when a young teen recognized us on the sidewalk and invited us to join a game of catch football. He'd been a referee on Tuesday nights and considered us friends. These small encounters left me feeling that I truly belonged where I lived.

It occurred to me that hockey might be the same kind of neighbourhood glue for others who'd taken part in those outdoor games, and my mind turned to the phenomenal energy of that Regent Park team, and of the busload of fans that had come along to both those outdoor tournaments, spending entire days in the freezing dampness.

One man's face held a place in my mind. We'd seen each other stalking back and forth while cheering on our teams. He seemed to preside over the group from Regent Park, kids and parents. He couldn't have been older than thirty-five, but I felt sure that if I looked into the program, I'd find him in charge.

Regent Park is among Toronto's poorest neighbourhoods. If the rest of the city pays any attention to it at all, it is usually due to a sensational crime story. It isn't necessarily where you'd expect to find a highly successful community-based hockey program.

I made some calls, and eventually learned that the man I was looking for was Dexter Slater. He'd moved to a different recreation department in the west end of Toronto by the time I caught up with him. We met in his office, off the corner of a community-centre gymnasium.

"I grew up in Regent Park. All my friends played hockey, and we spent our afternoons on the outdoor rinks, all winter long. There are two rinks in Regent—one south of Dundas Street and one north. I grew up on the south side, and it used to be that there was a great divide between the two. It bordered on racism, I guess. In North Regent there were traditional white families who had been there for years. If you were black or from anywhere else— Asian, Indian, any minority, really—you lived on the south side. It wasn't an economic divide, just a cultural one.

"There's no border now. It's kind of ironic, because eventually people got together and now the whole neighbourhood is racially mixed, but then it was real. My family came here from St. Vincent, in the Caribbean, when I was seven years old, so we lived on the south. But when we were kids, the one thing that would get us to cross Dundas was hockey.

"I was never much of a skater. The first time my friends said, 'Come on to the rink,' I didn't know what a rink was. I'd never seen ice before. When I first put on skates I spent most of the time falling down or holding on to the boards. But, like with anything else, it was just a matter of banging away at it. That's what my friends did and that's what I wanted to do. You know, none of us had a lot of money, but this was free, and it was huge to us.

"So, after I'd grown up, finished school and started working for Parks and Recreation, I saw I could give something back. The hockey program wasn't much. There was a huge influx of people to Regent from all over—a lot of southeast Asian families, kids who had no chance of ever playing hockey and whose parents could never afford to get them playing. I started looking for volunteers, and right away people were keen. They just needed someone to get it started.

"The big challenge was equipment. There are a couple of guys from Regent who are playing professionally. David Silverstone is one, and Trevor Daley is another. Their families helped us out, and so did the St. Mike's Majors, and we got huge funding from the Toronto Maple Leafs.

"We ended up with about a hundred kids. They'd arrive on Friday nights, all of them at once, and there was organized chaos getting them all sized and suited up. I mean, it's just a big, open space. Every inch of the floor was jammed with kids trying stuff on. You had the jocks going on backwards, the shoulder pads all over the place. I was overwhelmed. It was just me and a few paid staff. There is no way we could have done it without all the volunteers.

"For a family from Asia who have gone through all it takes to move to a new place where they don't speak the language, you know, they see hockey on TV, they see the pictures in the papers, and then they find out their kid wants to play hockey. Even if they have no understanding of the game, they know that hockey makes you as close to being Canadian as you can get.

"When I first started working at the city I heard a lot of stuff about Regent. 'Well, we'll invite Regent to the tournament, but they probably won't show.' Or 'If they show up, they're just going to fight. You can't control them.' It was kind of a joke. So, once we got started I was thinking, 'Okay, that's going to change.' We had something to prove.

"We became a force to be reckoned with. For a couple of years there, the final for the city-wide tournament was played in Maple Leaf Gardens. One year we lost in overtime, and another year we won, but either way the Regent team left with its head high. We earned that respect. The name alone—Regent—has all kinds of connotations in Toronto. For a Regent team to do this. I mean, can you imagine, for those kids and their parents? Maple Leaf Gardens? It was enormous."

Dexter said his family has moved away from Regent Park now. He still gets together with some of his childhood pals to play. A few of them are in a men's league on Thursday nights, and he comes out once in a while.

"I'm still not a great skater—I'm what you'd call a real ankle-burner. But nobody minds. It's a good time.

"But I haven't been out as much lately," he told me, and his face filled with pride as he turned his computer screen so that I could see the image that was on his desktop: a six-month-old baby.

"I've got other things to think about."

* * *

Pride is beginning to wear thin among the Leaside Flames select team, on the visitor's bench in this arena in North York. We have rules regarding on-bench behaviour—rules that were set down and agreed to at the very first practice: no negative talk between players on the bench, and no comments about what is happening on the ice.

So far, even in a losing game like this one, it seems to be sticking. The boys know they can all use whatever support there is. So when I open the gate and let someone off the ice, even if they have just fanned on a shot, dropped a pass on to the other team's stick, or stumbled while trying to turn around, I won't say anything about that, and neither will anyone else.

Two months ago, when we held tryouts for this team, there were three or four players who were below the calibre of the rest. Calling them to tell them they hadn't made the team was far from easy, but in most cases, neither the child nor the parents were very surprised. When we got to our final tryout, we had eighteen players left to choose from: two goalies, six defence and ten forwards. The problem was that ten forwards were too many. Nine forwards makes three lines—a centre and two wingers on each. We needed to make one more cut. And in the end, it came down to two players for one slot, and one of those players was Derek, Guy's son.

Derek's weakness was his skating. He had drive, great puck-handling skills and a wonderful work ethic. I was certain he was the right choice, as was Roman, because we'd both seen him play for years and knew that his attitude would invariably make up for whatever was lacking in his skating. But a tryout is a tryout. If I were another kid's parent and saw a spot on the team go to somebody who didn't skate as well as my kid, I'd be upset.

With only thirty minutes of ice time left, there still wasn't a clear choice, so we held a little game. We'd spent the previous four tryouts doing drills that tested skating speed and skill, fitness, puck-handling and willingness to work, but we hadn't let the kids really play. In that thirty minutes, Derek made the team. He showed grit and energy, and seemed to have a natural sense of where to be, even if his skating could only barely get him there.

I have never regretted our decision, but right now, as we're entering the last bit of this game, Derek is looking tired. He's been out for at least two minutes, and he needs a rest. I keep calling to him, but I can't get him off. He's playing on the far wing, all the way across this expanse of ice, and the longer he stays out there, the longer it's going to take him to get his tired self over here. So, up and down the wing he goes: arms pumping and head swinging, back and forth, trying to get the puck firmly away from the other team.

"Derek!" I'm calling. "Derek! Change! Change!"

The head nods, the arms go, the puck gets dumped back into our end, and poor Derek chases after it again.

When a team breaks down under pressure, players forget what they know. They scramble and chase and make heroic lunges that only make things worse, and once that downward spiral starts, it's just a matter of time until the puck is in the wrong net.

We can't get the puck out. The other team has kept at us for going on three minutes now and Matti, our goalie, is stopping shot after shot while the other team's fans roar with excitement. Dave and I are calling for someone to just dump the puck away.

I can see Derek calculating how long it will take his man to get to the puck, and whether he can get off the ice first. The answer is no. I have now stopped calling him off, and am only hoping for a break in the play. But before that can happen, Derek apparently decides it is time and, head down, charges in our direction.

The defenceman he was covering sees what is happening and calls for the puck. There's nothing now between him and our goalie. We are all—Dave, me, Roman and the parents—holding up our hands yelling "Derek! Stop! Derek! Go back!"

He ignores us. He's watching the play as he comes off, and, remarkably, in the midst of the mayhem, one of our defencemen, Taylor, is watching him.

Taylor somehow finds the puck in heavy traffic, and instead of dumping it off the boards and down the ice, he manages a little chip through the middle that bounces off several pairs of skates and lands about five feet in front of Derek, all by himself, with nothing but all of Siberia between himself and the other team's net.

It is a spectacular race. Exhausted Derek pulls every last stride out of his empty legs, while the other squad, like a team of stallions, gallops in pursuit. They're closing the gap by the half-second, but Derek has a very big lead, and in front of the net, he pulls a nifty fake and scores. Their poor goalie, who ten seconds ago was bored out of his mind, has now been brought down by the littlest kid on the woebegone other team.

We pull Matti in the last minute, and don't score, but we don't give up any more goals, either. We lose 4–3, but we greet the final buzzer with hoots and roars. It's as proud a celebration as any loser could dream of, and, at the very end, after the two lines of players have shaken hands and are coming off the ice, I'm holding the door open and saying "Well done!" not nearly often enough.

Wesley's the last off. He skates hard the last ten feet and leans into a snow-spraying stop before coming off.

He's beaming.

III

I WORK ON THE MORNING SHOW, *Music and Company,* on CBC Radio 2. I arrive at the station in time to go on the air after the news at 6:00 a.m., so I have to get up early—or, more accurately, early enough. The exact definition of "early enough" is something I've experimented with over the years. Suffice to say it is a time that makes it painful to stay up late too many nights in a row.

The schedule does have its advantages. For one, I finish work relatively early in the day. I do have to prepare for the next day's show, but if I do that at night from home, I can leave work in good time.

That's what I've been doing for the past month—getting home in good time to, well, to organize my things. There aren't many things in my life right now, so I find I can truly organize them all, and I have, every last one— pictures, kitchen supplies, books—more than once. I have put together my donated sound system and carefully organized it on the Ikea shelves so that none of the connecting cables between the components are visible from the room—a miracle of electrical routing and design. I can put on some music, sit in my armchair and look for cables. Last week, I saw two; today, none.

It is 12:30. I have had my lunch. In three hours, I will see Melissa when I pick her up from school. Her friend Ayesha will come with her to my place. They will tell me about their day. They will sit at the kitchen table and do homework while I fix them a snack, usually a bowl of cereal, and we will talk. Then I will take them to dance class. The subway ride there is one of my favourite things. We go to the front of the train and play a game in which we watch the track zooming by beneath our feet. The rule is that we must stare down at the tracks, without looking ahead, and allow ourselves to be surprised by the switches that lurch off into service yards and spurs, pulling our gaze with them before we bring ourselves back. We also play a game when we get off the train: Melissa and Ayesha run up the stairs and I take the escalator, and then, from the top, they count how many people get off the escalator before me, and claim to have won by that many points.

I never win.

Ayesha's mother, Angela, brings them home from dance, and I pick Melissa up from their home, and we get another half-hour together before I bring Melissa back to her mother's place for the night.

Then, after that, I will see Wesley at 8:30, when his Scout meeting finishes and I bring him home to his mother's, as well. It is a three-block journey and can take from ten minutes, at a reasonable speed with no diversions, to twenty-five, a miracle of delaying tactics on my part. On these Tuesday evenings I balance awareness of my son's need for sleep with my need to spend time with him. Sometimes we walk, but on very cold or snowy days, when I bring the car, it requires several trips around the block at exceedingly slow speeds to feel we've connected at all.

I find I am becoming acutely aware of what "connected" feels like, although I can't say how it works. Playing subway games does it for me with Melissa, as does being in the kitchen, washing dishes while she does her homework. With Wesley it is harder for me to predict. Sometimes we may have talked the entire way home from Scouts, but as I watch him go through the door at his mother's I feel overrun with emptiness and failure. Sometimes I think about that fifteen minutes for the sixteen hours preceding them, and still I walk home hollow. I am beginning to admit to myself that all of that thinking doesn't actually help, and might even make things worse.

Still, I am thinking about it again today. I am trying to remember that feeling of being connected to my children in a relaxed and unselfconscious way, but I can't. It is like the voice of a loved one who has died and whose everyday words and expressions are suddenly gone. I can almost hear it, almost remember how it feels to not have to think about it, almost, but not at all. In eight hours, I'll have fifteen minutes to find it again.

After that, well, maybe tomorrow.

. . .

The select team won Saturday night, against a very weak team—which, after all the hard digging of recent weeks, was almost a disappointment. Dave organized a tougher practice than usual that morning, and the team seemed to have internalized the pace he was asking for.

He has introduced the idea of an offence/defence switch. The game changes in a flash, he told us, and if players are going to take advantage of opportunities, they have to learn to flick a switch the moment the puck changes hands: offence—click—defence.

The main tool in this endeavour is a good, clean stop. Players may be tearing one way, but if they are going to make the switch effectively they have to be able to dig into the ice and instantaneously charge in the opposite direction.

The players raced diagonally across the width of the ice, stopping as close to the boards as possible before tearing off towards the other side. I dared to try it, last in line. Mine were cautious little stops, but I felt the beginnings of excitement in my legs, absorbing all of that forward-moving energy and releasing it in a burst going the other way. It was only a tingle, but the feeling keeps coming back. I've thought about it as I've leaned against the wall in the elevator at work, in the subway station, in line at the grocery store. It's worse in my kitchen on these long afternoons. I feel like jumping out of my own skin.

I try holding myself at an angle with a kitchen chair while I lean to one side, pushing my outside foot against the baseboard below the cupboard, emulating the position of a stop, but it is not the same. It wasn't the angle of the lean that was exciting on the ice, it was feeling all of my weight being pushed down through the bottom of my feet when I stopped.

I can remember my ankles not being as strong as I wanted them to be. I read in one of Roy MacGregor's books that when Guy Lafleur was a boy, he wore lead weights around his ankles when he went to school each day. I put books in a bag and try to lift them with my feet. I do this for ten minutes, then try to imagine a grinding stop on the ice and lean onto my kitchen chair again.

I still don't feel like Guy Lafleur.

I pace around the room, back and forth, in front of the neatly wired shelves. It's four whole days until the next select practice, and even then I don't really skate there. I need another place to skate. Ice time is expensive, I hear. For me to rent New Centre Ice for an hour would be crazy. I wouldn't even know how to best use the time. No . . .

It is a cold day. The puddles that lurked in the gutters just last week are solid now. The outdoor rinks have been open for a week. At Withrow Park, and according to the city schedule, the rink is booked for "Shinny Hockey—18 years and older," from now until 3:00 p.m.

My stomach tightens.

It is one thing to farm pucks on a rink full of ten-year-olds. Even if they can all outplay me, I still have longer legs and a shred of the authority that comes from being an adult. I am now contemplating playing with a group of grown men, who will watch me wobble onto the ice, rolling their eyes and wondering why I bother.

Still, I want to do it. I check the times again.

My skates are in the back room, in the bag I take to practices, along with my helmet, gloves and a bag of pucks.

I do some dishes. My legs ache. I wash a glass, then grab my hockey bag and head for the door before I can change my mind.

It's a short walk to the park. There *are* people playing, but only five. I am going to do this now, that much is clear, so I close off my thoughts and go about the task of tying my skates, pulling on my jersey and snapping on my helmet. Then I walk out of the chalet with my six-year-old Sher-Wood stick in my sixteen-year-old hockey gloves, my thirty-year-old second-hand skates on my feet, a puck in my pocket, and I'm on the ice.

One of the men is stickhandling in the other end; another is in the corner, holding onto the boards and huffing heavily. A guy in his mid-fifties, his cheeks flushed, is sitting on the bench, breathing out clouds of steam and smiling; and in this end, at the blue line, a mustachioed bear of a man has a line of pucks on the ice and is booming slap shots at the net.

I find a spot along the boards, near centre.

Dave always starts the select team's practices with skating circles—first counter-clockwise, then clockwise, making large figure eights and back again. That will do.

Turning counter-clockwise is good. It's the turn I know I can do. I can cross my right foot over my left and feel myself pick up speed as I go. I can lean into the turn and feel the push on the edge of my blades. There— that's what I imagined back in the kitchen. This is going well. I can do this. What was I worried about?

I turn that circle a couple more times, feeling strong, leaning harder before coming out of it at centre ice to go the other way. I start to lift my left foot and lean to my right when I feel my balance go. The same legs that were strong and secure leaning left are brittle and weak leaning right. I'm not sure I *can* lean this way. I straighten up and try again, still going quite fast, but I wobble even more. My right foot is wooden, my back goes tight and my arms swing stupidly. I need to stop, so I lean into my edges. My left foot rattles like a stick on a picket fence, my knees buckle and my legs fill with hardened panic as my hip hits the boards.

Apparently I don't know how to *stop* while facing to the right, either.

I am a few feet from the smiling guy on the bench.

"Been a while, eh?"

I smile and nod, and start off again, this time slowly.

I spend the next fifteen minutes turning clockwise, trying to be able to lean and cross one foot over the other. I find I've already coined a name for this exercise in my mind: a wrong-side turn. Not the most optimistic name, I know, but that's what this is for me—the wrong way to turn.

In that fifteen minutes there is one occasion when I realize I have leaned to the right, stepped across with my left, and pushed off again without wobbling. It is a satisfying moment.

I take the puck out of my pocket and try to stickhandle as I go—and almost plough right into another player. Keeping my head up and holding on to the puck is apparently too much to ask.

Smiley steps from the bench onto the ice. He dumps his stick at centre and launches into a beautiful wrong-side crossover turn that takes him all the way down and around the net, before he glides around the other way and back. His upper body is straight and square and his legs are churning while he leans in as if his edges could hold up the *Titanic*. It's a beautiful thing to watch, and I'm doing just that for a while—watching—before I realize the other four players are staring at me.

"You playing?" one asks, and I stare for another second before finally getting it. It's how you make teams. You drop your sticks in the middle and somebody gets down with their eyes shut and divides them into piles.

A bespectacled fellow does the honours, and I end up with Moustache and a guy who looks to be in his early twenties and whose skates are splayed out to the sides like flippers. The other team has the round-bellied, puffing guy, and the two players who are clearly the best on the ice: Glasses and Smiley. They are also, I gather from their talk, old friends, and I immediately question the honesty of the stick sorting.

They've got first puck.

The Puffer quickly passes to Smiley, who slides easily around Moustache and takes the puck along the boards at centre.

I take a defensive position, and realize what I probably should have been working on for the past fifteen minutes: skating backwards. It makes sense when you're playing defence. You can watch the guy with the puck and see most of the passes he might make—to Smiley, for example, who has just entered my field of vision at the blue line and looks, in his vintage Red Wings sweater, like an RRSP commercial or a spokesperson for a Tim Hortons senior's home. Glasses slides him the puck between the toes of my skates and the heel of my stick and I find that, although I can move backwards, adjusting my direction is another matter. Smiley puts on a tiny sprint and is around me without even trying.

I hear a clunk behind me, which I take to be the puck's impact on the back of the net, but then I realize it's not the right sound: not the zingy, high-pitched *bink* of the hollow metal net support, but the *clunk* of the puck hitting a stick. I turn to see my teammate, the one with the blades splayed out like duck feet, with the puck firmly on his stick. He pumps his legs—skate blades still close to flat on the ice, but moving quickly—and he's off.

Glasses and Smiley are drifting gracefully around our net and don't see how quickly he's charging. By the time they react, he's across their blue line, and the Puffer, sensing he might be able to handle this one, lunges, but to no avail. My teammate easily swoops the puck out of reach, chops his flipper-feet around the defence and scores.

There is no celebration. A big, toothy grin breaks out above his fuzzy, semi-bearded chin, and the game's back on. And this time, Glasses scores.

No one keeps track. We score, they score, and on it goes. Sometime later I manage an assist by bouncing the puck off the boards in a panic and having it land in front of the guy with the splayed feet. He scores.

"Nice goal." I say.

He says nothing, but smiles.

"What's your name?" I ask.

He makes a gesture with his hands to say that he can't speak—or can't hear, I'm not sure which. But he stops, mid-game, to bend down to the ice and write the name "Terry" with his gloved finger in the snow that has built up there.

I tell him my name. We shake hands and play on.

I try to get him the puck, without much success, but he still does all right. Once, later on, he sends the puck towards the net from a long way out, and it glances off

the Puffer's skate to me on the far side. I manage to cor-
ral the puck in time to shoot from about ten feet out into
the empty net. Terry smiles broadly from across the rink
and raises his stick.

A few minutes later, Terry waves and heads off into
the chalet. I check the time. It's 2:30. I've been playing
for an hour. I'm dead. As I walk home, my stomach is still
turning, but my legs are buzzing and I know I've done
something that I'm going to do again.

. . .

At 8:30 I hug Melissa on the sidewalk and watch as she
goes to the door before I run the three blocks to Wesley's
Scout meeting. It is a clear, cold night, a nice night for a
walk, but not a walk that will take much longer than necessary. We talk about school, about Scouts, about a
television show he watched that day. We're a half block
away when I tell him about my afternoon.

"I played shinny down at Withrow today."

"Hey!" he says, sounding mildly hurt. "How come you
didn't bring me?"

I am taken aback for a moment. It's not the reaction
I expected.

"Um . . ." I stammer. "It was during school."

"Oh."

He weighs whether that should matter, and as he does
I feel the emptiness of a lost moment descend into my
stomach. I want him to ask how I did on the ice—if my

stopping improved, how my wrong-side turns are coming, whether I still suck. I want all that to matter as much to him as it did to me. I want him to know that when I'm skating, I'm with him, even though I'm not. I want him to feel the same pride in me that I feel in him.

I have no idea if he feels any of that.

"See you, Dad," he says.

He hugs me stiffly, skips up the steps onto the porch and disappears inside.

## IV

IT'S 6:55 P.M. WESLEY AND I are in heavy traffic, still at
least ten minutes from Downsview Arena in northwest
Toronto. The game starts at 7:00.

The team policy is that all players must be at the
arena, fully dressed, thirty minutes before game time. A
late arrival is, at the coaching staff's discretion, justifica-
tion for a one-game suspension.

So far we haven't had to enforce this rule. I say "we"
meaning the coaches, including me, even though I'm the
one currently out of order by twenty-five minutes and
counting. Thirty minutes' grace time is not usually an
unreasonable expectation, but jammed and motionless
highways, packed side streets, freezing rain, and big, mul-
tiple-vehicle accidents blocking entire intersections
aren't the usual conditions. Not that horrendous traffic
in Toronto is unusual, especially not anytime between,

say, six in the morning and ten at night, but even by this city's standards, this traffic is vile. Already in the past quarter hour I have seen several drivers pound the horn and lean out their windows, saying words their children didn't know they knew.

I, too, am reaching new thresholds of stress behind the wheel. Making myself late is one thing, but causing my son to miss a hockey game is another. I am at the very edge of the seat, hands clamped to the wheel, and I am watching a traffic light half a block away with more intensity than I would the Stanley Cup finals. It is green, yet the cars beneath it move not at all. Finally, as the light turns yellow, a taxi at the intersection rolls from halfway across to two-thirds, before the light turns red and Wesley and I both explode, even though we have watched this same red light appear and disappear at least eight times.

I don't know what I'm going to say to the other coaches when we get there.

Wesley only needs to put on his skates. He crawled back through the van half an hour ago, struggled to pull on his gear, and has since watched both the pregame chat and the opening face-off slip from our grasp.

"Dad," Wesley's voice pleads from behind me, "we've been driving for two hours and now I'm going to be suspended and miss the next game, too!"

"Well," I say in a measured voice, "we'll see. Let me just get past this truck." The word "truck" explodes out of my mouth like buckshot.

It's 7:00 and the line of taillights snakes ahead without a break for as far as I can see. On my right is a van, inching ahead. There's a space behind it; if I can just squeeze in . . . Hey, wait a minute. I know that driver.

The driver is Trish, Patrick's mother, and now I see Patrick in the back, dressed in his goalie gear, enormous leg pads and all, biting his lip. Three minutes later, as we finally bump past the red light of eternity, I see another car turn left into the lane beside us with Devlin and Sam in the back. I heave a sigh of relief. If this many of us are this late, there's a chance the game will have been delayed.

It is 7:10 when we roll into the Downsview Arena parking lot. Wesley is running for the arena doors before I turn off the ignition, and as I thunder across the lobby and down the corridor to our dressing room, I see through the tunnel to the ice that the game has not yet started. Wesley already has his skates on, and another parent is tying them for him, as Devlin and Sam burst in.

Wesley is on the bench with the game clock showing three minutes gone.

Hallelujah.

We are playing a team from Willowdale, also on the other side of the clogged and wretched 401. They, however, and their many, many fans were apparently on time, filling the arena with a fair amount of discontent. Luckily for us, the referee came from somewhere even farther away and arrived only moments before game time himself.

My pulse is racing and my hands are pale, but aside from that, as I wrench open the gate for a line change, I feel a surge of energy at having somehow avoided certain disaster and disappointment.

The adrenaline boost of the drive seems to help the players, too. Five minutes after he comes puffing in, Devlin, a determined and scrappy centre, shoves his way past the defence and more or less pushes the puck right through the goalie for the game's first goal. Just a few minutes later, Charlie, a quick and clever skater who reminds me of a ten-year-old Yvan Cournoyer, sprints in around from the wing and finds an opening in the lower corner. The noisy Willowdale crowd has begun muttering to itself.

Things have been going quite well for Wesley's team since Christmas. The select teams have been grouped into tiers and we've been placed in the lowest of three, among teams much closer to our level. In early December, after some discussion, we decided to enter the team in the annual St. Mike's Christmas Tournament. It's the kind of event that gives hockey a questionable profile in the minds of families not already run off their feet.

It began on Boxing Day with a game at 9:00 a.m. Given that what I crave most with my children right now is time when we can just be together and relax, waking up early on Boxing Day to crowd behind a hockey bench surrounded by hundreds of bellowing parents and siblings in a cold, echoing rink was hardly what I would have wished for.

Even so, it turned out to be time well spent.

THE GIFT OF THE GAME

The team had been playing together for three months, working on skating and puck handling, but also getting to know each other and learning to feel comfortable with their places on the team. As of mid-November Dave began working on the simplest patterns of puck movement—plays the team could use in the heat of the moment. The kids used the patterns first in drills, then in scrimmages, but when it came to game time we were always back where we'd started. Passes would fling from our end onto opposing players' sticks. The defence and wingers would collapse around their own net while sharpshooters from the other team enjoyed enough time to shoot, reconsider, offer the opportunity to a teammate, and still get around to shooting again.

Now, a responsible account of the thing that happened at the Christmas Tournament in St. Mike's arena at 9:10 or so on Boxing Day morning brings on the necessity of an author's disclaimer. I've recognized since I began writing this story that I was presented with the chance to brag with impunity about the brilliance of my son. I do not want to write such a book I have no interest in giving Wesley a backhanded boost that comes with the need to prove himself against what some deluded middle-aged puck farmer wrote about him all those years ago.

Having said that, I do feel obliged to write about that first great moment in the Christmas tournament.

The team was playing North Toronto, who were placed far above us in the standings. Dave told us all that, even though we were sacrificing a good deal of the winter holiday for these games, we really shouldn't expect to win. We would be playing much better teams in the hope of raising our level of play for the second half of the season.

That is not what happened. A coin dropped for our team in that game. The guys began looking at each other, seeing patterns, believing they could really do it, and proving to themselves more and more that they could.

It started with Wesley.

He'd already had many good moments in the season. He was leading the team in goals, some of those goals being the kind that have burned their way into my memory banks like finely crafted films.

It is only a year since the outdoor tournament at Giovanni Caboto, when Wesley, Derek and Ben played so courageously—and hopelessly—against that inexorable Regent Park team. In that game Wesley was given a penalty shot and failed to raise the puck. He talked about wanting to be able to shoot "top shelf" for months afterward, and sometime over the past couple of months it stopped being talk.

He's also been playing well with his linemates. Wesley usually plays centre, and while we haven't settled on a left winger, the right winger is almost always a soft-spoken boy named Nathan. They play on the same team in house league. Nathan isn't the fastest skater, and doesn't have the hardest shot, but Wesley loves playing with him. He is smart, generous, persistent and has a good eye for a well-timed pass.

Wayne Gretzky left behind some sixty records when he retired, but there is one that is a gift to coaches. The game's most celebrated player scored 1,016 goals and more than double that in assists: 2,222. More than twice as often, when Gretzky's team got the puck in the net, it wasn't because he'd skated around all the other guys but because he'd seen someone else in a better position and passed.

I'm told that for coaches at the "AAA" level, getting kids to pass the puck is next to impossible. Most of the players who get that far, that young, learned long ago that there is no point in giving the puck to someone else, because they will be less likely to know what to do with it. At the elite levels, the ability to see and understand the power of a well-placed pass comes very late in a player's development and sometimes doesn't show up at all.

This year's Leaside atom select team doesn't have that problem. The play that started their wonderful Boxing Day experience was the oldest passing play in the book: a give-and-go. Wesley had the puck in the corner to the side of the North Toronto net. He saw Nathan along the boards, and as the North Toronto defenceman rushed, Wesley passed to Nathan and charged for the net. Nathan got the puck, waited a beat for the same defence-man to stop and come for him, then passed it back to Wes, now in front of the net, and Wesley scored.

We—Dave, Roman and I, the whole team, all the parents—went berserk. For those few seconds our team completely controlled the flow of the game. With a sim-ple pass-go-pass pattern, our team made the leap from a team full of heart but not really in contention to a group of players that could do what they needed, when they needed, and make it look easy.

From that moment on, it was as if our players saw patterns upon patterns every time they got the puck.

When things are going badly for a team, its players tend to see less and less. It's not that anyone plays any worse, but that opportunities go unnoticed and fall to the other team. When a team's vision is opened up, when they begin to see each other and see possibilities, chances spring out of the ice. All of a sudden our wingers were seeing their defencemen waiting at the blue line and were passing back to them, opening up the game and creating plays they wouldn't have dreamt of mere minutes before.

Our second goaltender, Patrick, emerged as a formi-dable force in that game. Accepting Patrick onto the team was, as it had been with Derek, a calculated risk. Patrick only began skating a couple of years ago. He is a big lad, and if there was a problem with his goaltending, it was with his agility, his ability to move quickly up and down and from side to side. He proved in his first game that those concerns were unfounded, but two months later, on Boxing Day morning, he made it hard to believe there had ever been any question. Time after time Patrick came up with the puck when nobody, least of all the guy who just took the shot, thought he could.

* * *

"We were just over the moon when Patrick made the select team." Trish, Patrick's mother, told me. "It was a pretty overwhelming feeling for us. He was a late learner when it came to skating, so we really thought it was impossible because of his visual disability."

His what?

"We had him tested and [he was] labelled with a learning disability, and they discovered a visual-perception disability as well. The learning disability means there's a big difference between his verbal ability and his ability to write those same ideas down, but the visual-perception thing is purely physical. They had an occupational therapist working with him, and he was having trouble catching a ball or riding a bike. He has poor trunk muscles, so they told us he wouldn't be able to get up and down very easily."

I was having trouble believing we were talking about the same Patrick.

"They told us to forget about team sports, and not to worry about it. 'He'll swim or run,' the psychologist told us, 'but it wouldn't be fair to expect anything else.' It still blows my mind every time he makes a save," Trish said. "Hockey—I mean, *goaltending*—it was out of the question."

So, was the diagnosis wrong?

"No. He has a visual-perception disability."

Then, how is he doing it?

"We can't explain it. He shouldn't be able to, but there it is—he's doing it. Somehow, he's compensating.

"I still find it incredibly stressful to see him out there. I mean, I'd never tell him this, because he comes off the ice just beaming every time, and meanwhile I'm a nervous wreck. Sometimes, if the other teams get by the defence and there are two or three of them coming in on Patrick, I just can't stand it. But he's fine with it. 'Bring it on,' he says. 'The more pressure the better.' I'm practically beside myself.

"There's no hockey at all in my family. We're Irish. My father came to Canada forty-three years ago and only last year bought his first pair of winter boots. We're really not winter people. In fact, if there was one place in sport where we would have pushed Patrick, it was soccer, but he's taken to hockey."

There's another reason hockey has become important for Patrick.

"Patrick lost his father when he was in senior kindergarten. It was an enormous blow. I had no idea where we were going for a while. That's one reason soccer worked—it was affordable for a single mother. My father helped out a lot. He got up early with Patrick and took him to school. They forged a real bond. But then, a few years ago, David came into my life, and it was David who urged Patrick to try hockey."

So, David came with a hockey background, then?

"Oh, no! He's Irish, too. He plays Irish football. He had to learn everything about hockey on his own so he and Patrick would have something to talk about on the way to and from games. It's worked like a charm. There are furious ball hockey games on our driveway now, and Andrew, our three-year-old, is picking it up.

"Patrick's had enough struggles in his life. We don't ever put pressure on with hockey. If he thinks he's had a bad game, David lets him figure out what to do about it. He works hard in school, but it's a struggle. Hockey is something that is really *his,* that he's good at and no one else in the family is. It makes him feel fantastic."

Trish watched the Christmas tournament as she always does: from the back of the stands, playing "phantom goalie," as she called it—wincing, moving, gasping, living save after save right along with him. David was there, with Andrew, the three-year-old, tearing around the stands between his parents, and so was Patrick's grandpa—Trish's father—who'd spent so many early mornings with Patrick.

He leaned over to Trish at one point after Patrick had kicked away a low shot and pounced on a loose puck.

"I wish I knew where that psychologist is now," Patrick's grandpa said under his breath to Trish. "Biggest waste of money."

• • •

In the end, North Toronto won that game, which they should have done. They were seeded at the top of the first tier and we were near the middle of the third, but for our players, things had changed. They had seen and felt how easy it was to be fully in control, to think quickly and act decisively—to make the game theirs.

That was just over two weeks ago. The team won its first league game after that tournament, and by the end of the first period against Willowdale, having braved the worst of Toronto's traffic misery on the way, we are going into the second period with a 2–0 lead.

Winning is still a new feeling for this team, and the players tighten up, unsure of what to do next. The game is tied by the end of the second period, and although no one looks particularly stressed, there is a feeling on the bench that it would be an awful shame to let this one get away.

At the start of the third period Dave puts on the line we've started calling the Wrecking Crew*: Derek, James and Devlin.

They send the other team back onto their heels and two minutes later, when Wesley, Nathan and Andrew pour onto the ice and the momentum is palpable.

The Willowdale team ignores that though, and moments later has three players bearing down across the blue line. Their winger manages a hard shot, but Patrick handles it easily and kicks the puck out to Reed, who is playing left defence.

Reed is Dave's son. He carries the puck a few strides

*For the record, the other two forward lines eventually earned nicknames, as well. Charlie, Shawn and Alex became the Mystery Line when they arrived so late for a game that the lineup remained a mystery until the last second. Wesley, Nathan and Andrew were the Untamed Foo-Foos. The name was Shawn's idea. I never understood exactly where it came from, but the team enjoyed chanting "Foo! Foo! Foo!" when they took the ice.

towards the boards and looks up. It isn't a long look. There is a Willowdale winger coming hard at him, but Reed doesn't hurry. He sees Nathan ahead of him along the left boards, sees his defence partner, Sam, starting out in front of the net. He looks at Nathan again, back to Sam, and then sees Wesley near centre. Then, unbelievably, he waits yet another beat, until the Willowdale guy is almost on top of him, before sliding the puck through a narrow corridor of players, all the way to Wesley, already on the move.

In an instant, Wesley has taken the puck wide to the boards and is crossing the blue line, only one defender between him and the Willowdale net. All he has to do is deke one player. There is one collective inhalation of breath as he reaches the Willowdale defenceman, but in that instant he fools us, his teammates, *and* that lone defence-man. Wesley doesn't deke. He doesn't weave or lurch. He doesn't do anything at all. He just stops carrying the puck, leaving it drifting where it is, and he skates on to the net.

The defender hesitates, the crowd goes silent, the Willowdale goalie relaxes just a fraction and Andrew, trailing four strides behind, picks up the orphaned puck and drills a beautiful wrist shot under the goalie's blocker to score.

Leaside hangs on, and we whoop all the way to the dressing room. Dave praises everybody's good work, pointing out that the solid goaltending, the smart defence, the clean passing and the persistent forwards all had as much to do with the result as that one moment we are all still talking about fifteen minutes later.

"How did you know he was there?" Dave finally asks Wesley, speaking for all of us. "I didn't see you look at all. *I* didn't even notice Andrew. How did you know he was there?"

"I snuck a look when I was at centre," Wesley says, smiling in an embarrassed way.

We pack up, good feeling still swimming around the lobby as we go, and are soon back on the road, the traffic smooth and peaceful, northwest Toronto glowing contentedly around us.

We are on the road a while before he says it.

"Dad," I hear him say as I'm changing lanes to head south. "You know back there when Dave asked me in front of everyone, I said I looked back at centre and saw Andrew? But I didn't, really. I said that because I was embarrassed, but I didn't look. I don't know how I knew Andrew was there. I just knew."

He seems as puzzled about this as he does happy, but I have nothing more to say. I tell him again that what he did was a wonderful thing, no matter how he did it. I tell him he was great.

He *was* great, too. There's nothing in it for me to be proud of him. Whatever he did on the ice was nothing to do with me. It's his and his alone—the ten-year-old in the back seat behind me, reliving that moment, seeing it happen, feeling that thrill again and again and again.

He doesn't tell me he's doing that, but I know he is. I don't have to look. I just know.

v

SHINNY THIS AFTERNOON IS AT Dieppe Park in East York. It's a twenty-minute walk, and I do it today as I usually do: with my equipment bag looped by the handles over my hockey stick, and the stick slung over my shoulder like a woodsman's axe.

It's a new stick. When I really looked at the old Sher-Wood I saw it was in pretty rough shape—the blade had a big chunk torn out of the bottom. So I bought myself a new one as a gift at Christmas. Actually, I bought two. The big-box store at the mall was advertising a "second stick half price" sale, so I bought two: a cheap one, and a very nice "Featherlite" with a Paul Coffey curve. I was even slightly embarrassed to have it standing in the corner of the living room on Christmas morning.

But that was two months ago. Today, I can admit to feeling some pride as I walk to the rink, parading myself in this way. I have taken on a role in this game, and clearly, even though it is a modest one, I am beginning to feel that I have earned it.

Players take on roles in every hockey game, I've begun to see, and they are more or less consistent from rink to rink. The irony is that in shinny games, when positions aren't assigned and people find their own way of fitting in, player roles seem to be even more tightly cast.

The entry-level role is that of the Wobbler, who is happy just to be on skates at all and who rarely gets involved in the play. Until recently, that was me. But as the season has rolled on, I've begun to see that I've made sufficient progress to climb up a notch. I am not always the worst player out there anymore. I sometimes see things happening in a way that allows me to react in time to do something about them. I've become a Digger.

There are many levels of Diggers, but all share one quality. A Digger is anyone whose level of effort exceeds their level of skill. There are very good Diggers, and some not so, but the trick is to hang onto the role even when the pressure increases. Some Diggers, when outclassed, become Hackers, while others take a lateral step and become Clowns. On the other hand, if a Digger finds that he has a generally higher skill level than most of the others playing, he can pull out what tricks he has—the dipsy-doodle behind-the-back off-the-skate deke, or the shifty show-off head fake—and thereby take on the higher role of Hotshot.

And for each of these players—the Digger, the Hacker, the Hotshot, the Clown—there is yet another choice. The Hacker who won't stop hacking, the Digger who digs pointlessly, the Clown who won't shut up, the Hotshot who celebrates just a little too much, all have the option of making the remarkably short trip from their usual role to that of Asshole. Unfortunately, when one player makes the switch, it's not unusual for everybody to follow.

At that point, the game has become something nobody wants any part of. There is, however, one other stock character at shinny games whose presence will diffuse the situation, and that is the Journeyman.

The Journeyman has dekes he never uses and is neither young nor old, but he is the envy of both. He is tolerant of the Wobblers, can disarm the Hotshots and elevates the Diggers into potential Journeymen themselves. When the Journeyman includes you in his game, you feel lucky to be where you are, and you act accordingly.

I'm not sure he has any idea, but it has become clear to me that in most of the select games, when he's able to do what he can, Wesley, at the ripe old age of ten, is a Journeyman. I think of that these afternoons as I'm pushing at the puck along the boards, trying to dig it out from between my skates or even just as I'm warming up, turning circles. I'm not imagining Wesley and me in the same game, exactly, but the image never leaves my mind, either. I see myself as the kid, awkward, frustrated and uneven, surprised by what modest success comes along, while my son, his hands as steady as granite, his head up, his stride smooth and long, roams the ice with absolute authority.

My favourite shinny games are the weekday afternoon games at Dieppe Park. There aren't usually more than ten people playing, and there is a nice balance of players. The Sunday games, like today, are more crowded, but still tend to move along nicely. Players come and go, and most Sundays, by the late afternoon, there is a small number who are clearly in for the long haul.

I am tired and could have stayed home today, but I pushed myself to come out. It's quite cold, but even so it is the end of winter as far as shinny hockey is concerned. The temperature could plummet from now until Easter, but that wouldn't change a thing. Today is the last day that Toronto's outdoor rinks will be open for this year.

Shinny has become an important part of my life. I've decided to treat today as a wrap-up of sorts, to take stock of what I've learned and to set goals for whatever ice time I may find between now and next December, which seems like a very, very long way away.

Dieppe has a hockey area, complete with boards, benches and nets, as well as an adjacent skating pad, almost as large, which is reserved for pleasure skating. It gives the place a friendlier feeling, with families, sweethearts and young teens holding hands, giggling and shrieking as they play tag and crack-the-whip, while next door, caged within chain-link, the national game rages on.

There is a game in progress with a full complement of players as I take the ice, so I skate to the bench and join two others already there. Dealing with a surplus of players is also something that varies from game to game. Sometimes there are three full teams, with the third switching every two or three goals, the winners staying on. Other times players simply come off when they are tired.

I don't know what is happening in this game, so I wait to see what the two before me do.

They do nothing. They say nothing.

"Are you waiting to play, or should I just join in?" I finally ask.

"Just about," one says, looking at nothing, and meaning what, exactly, I still don't know.

I'm not sure what it is about sports and guys, but the old cliché about nobody saying any more than they have to, in my experience, is not a cliché at all. Those ridiculous rinkside television interviews, in which stock questions hang until the sweaty guy *du jour* hauls out a non-answer and heads to the showers, are merely the elevation of what happens at every level of play, in every arena, all the way down to pickup shinny at Dieppe Park.

I'm on the verge of committing the ultimate faux pas between men of sport—asking for more information—when the guys on the ice do stop playing. There's a break of sorts, during which I fit in a few skating drills, and then it's time to pile the sticks in the middle and start again.

No one says anything about what to do with the extra players, and we end up with eight on each team. I'm certainly not about to start talking about it, so we all stake out our square foot of ice and the game begins.

With so many playing, I find I can either hang back, getting involved only when the play comes my way, or get out front and compete with the crowd on both teams for a chance to get the puck. I opt to play back, seeing more action as the afternoon passes and some players rest, while others leave.

I'm not doing badly. I even score a couple of times, getting around a Wobbler on defence and making the turn in time to stuff in the puck. After my second goal, though, one of their better players hangs back to help out, and that's the end of my streak.

One of my teammates is a Journeyman of sorts. He's tall, with a good skating style and a long reach. He takes a pass from one of our defencemen and starts up the opposite wing. Two of the other team's better players are covering him, and although he still has the puck, it's clear he won't be able to keep it for long.

He looks up, his eyes meet mine and suddenly I get it. He's going to pass to me. I need to get myself to where the other players aren't.

This may sound like something I might have understood before, especially given that I've been helping to coach a select team in various passing drills for several months, but this is different. I have tried to pass or receive passes, but only in the rare moments when I can take my attention away from the very basic issue of being able to move in a way that allows me to be part of the game. Apparently, I've evolved, and I am finally seeing firsthand how it really works.

I tear to centre ice, all but yelling for the puck. The Journeyman is looking at me, but not passing. He finally dumps the puck back along the boards behind him. I feel wounded for a moment, until I notice the other team's Hotshot about ten feet to my right, waiting for what surely would have been easy pickings. The Journeyman didn't pass because it never would have gotten to me.

I feel the dawning of a great wisdom. For the rest of the game, I am all about the pass.

The Journeyman gets a couple of passes to me, well timed and well directed, but they bounce off my stick like hailstones off a tin roof. Like everything in hockey, this simple and elegant concept is far more difficult than it seems. The puck is hard, and if it's travelling fast, it bounces. If it's not travelling fast, it ends up on a stick belonging to the other team. I get a chance to return a pass to a teammate, and the puck, way off target, goes neatly onto the stick of the other team's Journeyman, who is now calmly streaming towards our net.

There is an almost audible nod among the others, and I know I've identified myself as a stock character I didn't even know existed until this moment: the Klutz. The Klutz throws himself into the game, sensing none of the subtleties being transmitted by his teammates, and, with galling efficiency, singlehandedly makes chaos out of order.

A Klutz who has fallen in love with the pass is a sorry fellow, indeed. I try to compensate for my failings, but I don't get many opportunities after that. The others have now seen what will happen if I'm involved in a passing play, and after a time I am only touching the puck when I go and get it myself. It's a terrible feeling. I leave the ice.

I find a place to sit along one of the benches and watch the activity around me in the chalet at Dieppe Park. It is getting late in the afternoon. Families are packing up for home, for Sunday dinners, kids tired and happy, fathers untying skates.

My children are with their mother on Sundays. I haven't had a Sunday dinner with them for months. I haven't seen them in almost twenty-four hours and won't see them for another forty-eight. I don't know what they did last night. I don't know what they are doing today, where they are right now, or where they will be; what is bothering them, what makes them happy or what they are hoping for in the days to come. It's as if they have left my life completely, as if, for these three days, we are not a family at all. I could call them, but with leaden tension filling the air between our homes, they will say they are fine and silence will drown our conversation, my yearning for them just another bad pass, sailing past and drifting nowhere.

I head back to the ice. The game I left ten minutes ago, the one where I established myself as a Klutz, has broken up. There are only two players on the ice now. The sun has all but set behind the houses around the park, and the grey evening light of winter has hardened along with a bitter wind that is sweeping across the ice. I try my skating drills, telling myself it is my last chance for months, but my focus is gone. My crossovers are clunky, I almost fall skating backwards, and I resort to turning the easy way, faster and faster, like a big dog chasing its tail.

Two more players arrive. They wear matching team jackets that are black and sleek with bold colours and a gold-embroidered "AA" on the sleeves.

They pass the puck around for a few minutes, easily turning power turns, sprinting from the corners and shooting casually at the open net, hard shots ringing off the crossbar.

One turns to centre and approaches me.

"How about you three verse* us?" he asks.

I look at the other two players, who have now drifted to either side of me. One is a Wobbler, through and through, the other a Digger with possibly as much skill as me, and both are somewhere well north of thirty-five, probably forty.

"Sure," I say, knowing we will not fare well, but not willing to give up the challenge or the chance to play. We pull the nets closer to centre, reducing the size of the game, and we're off. They get first puck.

I try a defensive position first, hoping to pick off their passes, but I am nowhere close. The puck floats between my legs, in front of my stick but out of my reach, behind my back, turning me around like a corkscrew. Theirs are beautiful passes, fast and smooth. The puck travels

---

*This has become schoolyard and arena vernacular. It is the verb form of "versus." I've heard it used in the past imperfect, too: "First we versed them, then they versed the other team."

silently from stick to stick. Without a word between them, these two show me exactly why hockey players don't talk. They're already communicating. The passes they send connect them to each other in a way words could never do. It is at once preverbal and highly sophisticated—a language of action, speed and intuition that I can't begin to speak.

Another pass slips past me to the right, and the taller of the two players, cradling the puck again just beyond my reach, drills it into the high corner of our net with such confidence that it seems the play could never have ended any other way.

I am already the fool in this contest, but I will not admit it. *I can do this*, I tell myself, my breath tightening, and I try again. I look for one of my teammates to pass to, hoping to catch my opponents out of position, but it never happens. They are too fast, too smart, and they are enjoying it. They love this language. It is an inside joke at my expense, and they will keep telling it again and again. They laugh. They swagger. They prance.

I feel my anger harden low. I may not be able to play with them, but I can stop their game. I am bigger than both of them.

I pick the smaller one and, using my size and what speed I have, aggressively come between him and his partner. It works initially, but at this pitch my lack of skill and restraint are a volatile mix and I begin to play harder, thinking less and less about who and what is in my way. In the tiny moments I have to react to their play, I hear myself deciding to do whatever it takes to stop them. They play faster, their circles tighter, passes crisper. I charge harder, my skates chopping at the ice. I am falling behind my man, but can still reach his stick with mine and jerk it away from the puck. He stops hard to turn and retrieve it, but I don't stop. I launch myself into him before shoving him aside and grabbing the puck to charge their net. His teammate is before me, but I wind up and whale at the puck before he can react. The puck sails upward and he leaps aside.

I miss the net.

I start for the puck, but as I do I can feel things have changed. The other players, including those on my team, are eyeing me warily. I feel a rush of shame, mutter something about having to go, and trudge off the ice.

I am still seething as I head to the men's room to collect myself. I was on the verge of playing with more violence still, I realize, and am glad that I left when I did.

The skating guards are out on the ice, dragging in the nets. The rink is closed. The season is over.

My two opponents come in and sit side by side across the room, not looking at me. They are much smaller than they seemed on the ice. They take off their helmets and I am stunned.

They are kids. Really. They are thirteen years old, maybe younger. Barely older than Wesley and his friends. They are skinny children with high voices and fresh, clean skin. They look scared, too, pretending to talk comfortably but glancing this way and that, wondering, I'm guessing, what would make a man their father's age behave like a schoolyard thug.

I slow down in my efforts to untie my skates. I don't want to leave at the same time as they do, to have to hold the door and possibly meet their gaze.

Ten minutes later, the chalet empty, I walk across the parking lot and out to the sidewalk, my stick—the cheap one—across my shoulder. Light from living rooms in the houses along the way pours out onto the lawns beside me. I can see figures inside that could be families gathered, but it's cold and the curtains are pulled shut. The only sounds I hear are the clunk of my boots and the rumble of the passing traffic.

# VI

IT'S EARLY MAY. The only hockey left is the kind on TV.

The select team finished under .500 for the year. There were one or two games we might have won and didn't, but several more that were never within our grasp. One crucial game in late February was against the team just ahead of us in the standings. If we'd won, we would have finished in fifth place overall. We didn't win, even though Dave, Roman and I all thought we could have. That put us in sixth place at the end of the season. On top of giving us a fairly dismal-sounding finish, it gave us an unfortunate spot in the playoffs.

The first round consisted of a two-game series. The second-place team played the fifth-place team, third played fourth, leaving us the unhappy job of meeting the team that had finished first.

The series was scheduled over March break, when a

third of our team was away. We were able to call up three players from the age group below ours, but they had their own playoff game to play first, at an arena somewhere across town. They arrived late, still sweating, and while we waited for them in the dressing room, the referee assessed a delay-of-game penalty. The other team started the game with a man advantage and scored. After that, our boys played bravely, but never came back.

The next game was two days later, right in the middle of the holiday week. Even fewer players showed. We lost 8–2. The select season was over.

Wesley's house-league season went on a few more weeks. He and Nathan played on the same line, passed and scored more than anyone else in the league, and their team finished in first place. But in the championship game, for whatever reason, the fire just wasn't there and they lost. The game finished late on a Sunday afternoon in early April. I found Wesley in the dressing room and mussed his sweaty hair. I told him he'd done well, which he had, and then said I'd see him Tuesday, which I would, and I went home.

That was it.

It was hard to believe at first. The hockey schedule at the centre of our lives for the past six months hadn't left much time for reflection. It was a life in motion in every sense—either moving on to the next drill, the next shift, the next scoring chance, or the next practice and the next game. Then, all of a sudden, hockey shifted from a central occupation to something we reminisced about when nothing else was going on—a memory bank of shared moments.

One of those moments sustained us more than the others.

The last regular-season game was against Downsview. The two teams had met twice before, and Leaside lost both games. The difference was one very strong player, who I've since learned was named Joseph. Twice in each game he had skated right through our whole team to score.

In this last game, Dave assigned Wesley the task of covering Joseph whenever he came on the ice. If Wesley could eliminate the threat of Joseph, the rest of the team could focus on what they might do to win.

The first period see-sawed with chances on both sides, but none fell to Joseph. There were times, I'll admit, when Wesley did not appear to me to be absolutely on top of Joseph, and I was sure he was going to waltz in as he'd done so many times, but it didn't happen. By the third period we were up 3–1.

A Downsview player dumped the puck towards our net before turning back to his bench. The puck wobbled slowly towards our goal. Matti, our goaltender, came out, took a stride, mistimed his swing, and the puck, still wobbling, went between his skates and, with barely enough momentum, into the net.

Downsview's fans exploded. Matti buried his face in his hands. Roman, Dave and I all looked at the clock. There were seven minutes left, far too much time to coast on a one-goal lead, especially against a rejuvenated team with a player who could tie it up on a moment's notice.

A couple of shifts later, Downsview sent Joseph out to take a face-off in our zone. I pushed Wesley's line onto the ice, looked again at the clock—four minutes left—and felt the tension rise in my chest.

After some jostling, the puck slipped out to centre ice. Joseph corralled it and looped around to come up the ice again. The entire Leaside bench and fans gasped nervously when Wesley charged the puck. It's hard to know if he was acting protectively, trying to eliminate a threat before it got started, or if he saw an opportunity for himself. Either way, it was risky. Had he missed, Joseph would be alone with all the time and room in the world.

Wesley didn't miss. He knocked the puck away, stepped around Joseph, picked it up on the other side, and made for the Downsview net.

I can still see him swooping around from the right wing, the player he was supposed to be guarding now trying to guard him. He drifted past the goalie with patience I still don't understand, drawing him out of the net, and then tucked the puck in high on the left side with a slow-motion backhand. By the time the puck was in the net, the goaltender had reached so far that he was sprawled on his stomach and out of the play. The other team's star, still just a stride behind, could only watch.

Wesley turned to the bench, glowing and brimming with joy. He looked so happy, so full, so filled up with himself.

We've talked about that moment often, Wesley and I, both of us replaying the film in our minds, debating the details of what happened and when. I'll admit, I have even brought that film forward in my mind—the swoop, the goal and Wesley's face—to sweep aside the maw of emptiness on those Tuesday nights, when once again I find myself walking away from a house I used to live in, and a woman I used to love, and the children whose hearts I feel beating in my bones with every walking step.

It's easy to edit the film in those times—not Wesley's part in it, but mine. The camera angle changes from my point of view on the bench, hand ready on the gate latch, craning over the boards to see. I see the play from on the ice; gliding forward, I still see Wesley coming round from the right. Then, watching from beside the Downsview goal, I see his concentration, waiting for the goalie to move, sliding the puck back. I see the light in his face as the puck arcs over and lands softly against the back of the net. And then he is yelling joyously, jumping into my arms, and I am with him.

* * *

One Saturday afternoon we were watching a TV show we'd both seen before, when Wesley turned to me and said, "Let's go to Just Hockey."

Just Hockey is one of east-end Toronto's hockey pro shops, and the one that is currently favoured by the brand-name conscious hockey consumer.

I've never been big on shopping. I become brain-dead in minutes and seek only to escape. I have long assumed, especially among men, that I am not alone in this. Out of a dressing room full of sweaty guys just off the ice, for example, one wouldn't expect many to jump up and applaud gleefully at the prospect of a trip to the mall.

After that Saturday, I am no longer certain of this. It was months until hockey season and the place was jammed, mostly with males. The skate section had three staff members shuttling full time between customers. The stick section had packs of kids, literally, picking up sticks and shafts and blades, weighing them, flexing them, handing them back and forth and discussing their merits, while another crowd had assembled in the back corner of the store, apparently there only to look at goalie equipment. Not to buy, but to look. There were sets of pads, blockers, gloves, armour and custom-made masks, all displayed in the ready position, as if Ed Belfour himself might step out of them and sign autographs.

Most remarkable to me in all of this were the consultants. At Just Hockey there are those who actually handle the merchandise and present it to the customers, and there are those who, it seems, have no more responsibility than to impart wisdom on the *concepts* of the gear being sold. The Skate Man strolls the display like a professor addressing a seminar. The Goalie Man fields questions like a Buddha, all the while stroking his beard. Even the skate-sharpening station gives the feeling of a modern-day smithy. The sharpening machines are housed open-concept, like the grill at an uptown eatery, while the bladewrights within read the lives of their subjects with deep understanding.

The busiest consultant on this day, however, was the Stick Man.

Hockey sticks have become something worth talking about in recent years. The wooden stick has been pushed aside by what is called a "composite," a hollow shaft made of aluminum, graphite, titanium, Kevlar or rubber, with glued-on wooden blades. They are much lighter than a wooden stick and offer a great deal more flex. The top-of-the-line models are one-piece affairs, the shaft and blade made entirely of composite materials.

Still, composites are not for everyone. One of the features of the NHL All-Star break is a skills competition. Players compete in tests of skating speed, agility, shot accuracy and shot speed. This year's hardest shot, for the fourth time in as many years, belonged to the veteran defenceman from the St. Louis Blues, Al MacInnis. He won with a phenomenal drive of 98.9 miles per hour, launched with a good old-fashioned wooden stick.

Not long after, the Blues' other star defenceman, Chris Pronger, was taking questions at a postgame press conference. One reporter praised his shooting and asked what he did to improve his slap shot. "Easy," he said. "I pass it to Al."

Hockey parents love Al MacInnis. The best wooden stick costs fifty dollars, slightly less than the cheapest composite. The one-piece composites are currently going for more than two hundred. Each.

They aren't indestructible, either.

"It's hard to snap a Synergy," the Stick Man tells Wesley, while a clutch of rapt preteens gazes on, speechless.

"Hard," I'm thinking, remembering the face on a hockey camp counsellor who had done just that, blowing a month's pay, "but not impossible."

The Stick Man leaves this thought unspoken. He gracefully wields a one-piece silver composite as if it were Obi-Wan Kenobi's light sabre.

"The Aramid/Graphite shaft is super-light, with a 75 flex all the way down to the Z-Carbon pro-stiff blade, giving the stick a balanced feel. The whole Synergy weighs 415 grams, and the elliptical low kick point delivers a lightning shot with an effortless swing."

"And," he might have added, "it can be yours for only $230, not including taxes."

He didn't say that, though. Just as Wesley reached out to grasp this thing of beauty and perfection, the Stick Man put it back in the rack.

"You guys really shouldn't be asking your parents for one, though." he said, folding his arms. "Only an adult will really feel the difference. You'd be just as well off with one of these." And he gestured to the fence line of dun-coloured wooden sticks, sucking in light and energy by their dullard presence alone.

It was a brilliant strategy. Wesley's urgent, unrequited love was now bursting from his heart, the object of his desire promising not only skill and admiration, but maturity and manhood itself.

Wesley spent the rest of our visit at the composite temple, his tongue roundly fondling the names they bore: Synergy, Ultra-Light, Z-Bubble, Tri-Flex, Typhoon, Octane, Response.

For my part, I was still slightly embarrassed by my Featherlite with the Paul Coffey curve, the one I'd bought myself for twenty-six bucks, even with the knowledge that I'd only done that because along with it came the Sher-Wood Pro for half-price, costing me $10.99. I had moved the Featherlite from the corner of my living room to the back room with the rest of my gear, but it still had the ribbon I'd tied around it Christmas morning, and I still hadn't used it. Considering my development, it seemed an indulgence, when the cheaper stick was still more than good enough.

When we arrived at Just Hockey that morning, workers were replacing the front door. The aluminum frame was mangled and bits of shattered glass were scattered around the front of the store. Late the night before, we learned, a gang of thieves stole a car, lined it up with Just Hockey's front entrance, and ploughed right through, ripping both doors off their hinges. Then, while the alarm system screamed, they pillaged the store.

They ignored the cash registers. They ignored the skates and the pads and the thousand-dollar goalie sets. They only wanted sticks. At one or two hundred dollars each, in a matter of minutes the thieves were getting away with tens of thousands of dollars' worth of merchandise. There was no tracing the sticks, and selling them off must have been easy, because the same thieves came back a few weeks later and did it again. After that, Just Hockey left a car parked across the door when they closed.

The smart hood sticks with sticks. Just like booze and cigarettes, in Canada, they're as good as cash.

We left Just Hockey empty-handed that day, and although we'd both been entertained by the fantasy of how much happiness a few choice items could bring, the flatness of the post-hockey spring rushed back in even before we'd left the parking lot.

• • •

I came into some hockey gear not long after that day, and it came absolutely free of charge. Protection that suited my level of play.

First, my friend Jan, who works with me at the CBC, bequeathed me his gear—in a green garbage bag—from his own hockey days ten years before. Then, remarkably, my former father-in-law, Eric, astonished me by doing the same. Eric has had a basement full of hockey gear for close to forty years. He outfits neighbourhood kids and trades in the stuff they've outgrown. It's as much a charity as a business, and, just as a rough guess, I wouldn't be surprised if there were thousands of parents who could say he kept their children safe—and kept *them* out of the hockey poorhouse.

Eric's stuff appeared, ostensibly as a birthday present, but wrapped in a beat-up hockey bag with no card. The kids told me he'd left it for me. I'm guessing Wesley told him I'd taken an interest in playing and Eric saw it as an olive branch he could live with. It showed great courage; and, for me, hockey became even more full of metaphor.

So, all of a sudden I had two sets of shoulder, elbow and shin pads, two pairs of hockey pants, two helmets, and even a couple of old jerseys and socks, right there in my back room, waiting.

A week later I was at the Leaside Arena, registering Wesley for the next year's season, when I saw a little sign announcing times for "Adult Men's Shinny."

Even in the winter, when I'd been going to the outdoor rinks for shinny two or three times a week, I still had to wrestle with myself every single time for the courage to go, to present myself to strangers, my inabilities on parade.

After two months away from the ice my skating was even worse, but the next Friday, stomach in knots, I dashed home from work, convinced myself all over again, and left for the rink with my usual shinny set-up: skates, gloves, helmet and stick.

The game had already started when I arrived, so I climbed through the stands to the bench and rushed to get my stuff on. When I was done, I looked up and saw it was my turn and jumped on the ice, but something was different. It took a second to sink in, but this wasn't like the outdoor shinny games. Everyone else was wearing full gear, and, I realized as a slap shot went ripping in from the blue line, the outdoor shinny rule about not raising the puck did not apply.

I felt naked. I finished a couple of shifts, staying very far away from anything close to a shot, then slid off the ice and went back home.

My gear was piled in the back room.

I emptied the bags onto the kitchen floor. I had helped Wesley dress dozens of times, but this was different, like trying to teach someone else to tie a necktie —everything is backward. I couldn't remember what went on first.

Then I remembered, and I needed to get in the car and go back to Just Hockey.

I didn't have a jock.

Jocks, too, it turned out, have changed in recent years. There are boxer shorts, Lycra bodysuits and cup-and-garter sets, all of them vaguely feminine. The bodysuits had the look of a dance outfit, and the cup-and-garter sets like vintage lingerie, but I had to wear *something* and the garter thingy was only twelve bucks.

I must have checked that the curtains were closed about ten times before I put it on, but after the jock, the socks, shin pads and pants were easy. The shoulder pads took some figuring, with their clasps and laces and holes all over the place, and getting the jersey on top of all that took some contortions, too. After twenty minutes or so, I was ready.

I walked around the apartment a few times, looked at myself in the mirror, my eyes peering out between the bars of my caged face, and I took it all off again, lined up and ready for shinny the next Friday. The last things in the bag were my skates, almost as old as I am.

I looked at them again.

I'm not sure exactly where they came from or how many people have owned them, or even how old they really are. Eric gave them to me years ago, but they are exactly like the ones I got when my feet stopped growing in 1976—and they weren't new then.

I went back to Just Hockey.

It was still the midafternoon, and the church of hockey consumption was quiet. The various consultants had left their pulpits, and I was left on my own before the Great Wall of Skates. Easton, Graf, CCM, Nike—the cheapest pair I could find was over three hundred dollars.

The thing is, I knew I was going to buy something. Way back in January, when I first came here to get Wesley's skates sharpened and decided to have mine done, too, I began to wonder. The normally stoic sharpening guy picked up Wesley's and put them by the machine, then turned to mine and did something very close to a double take. He picked them up and looked at me with eyebrows reaching what used to be his hairline.

Still, three hundred bucks?

"You *need* these," my internal voice was saying, but not very convincingly. Another internal voice was saying, "Six months ago you couldn't turn to the right."

I left before it could go on any longer, and almost on its own, the car took me straight to Canadian Tire. The sporting-goods section was a shambles. And never mind consultants, I'm not sure there was anyone else in the store. I rooted around through the end-of-season leftovers, forced to admit that even a chump skater like me couldn't justify what I was considering here, even if it was only going to cost me sixty dollars.

Then I saw it: a lone CCM box on the top shelf. It wasn't torn, or bent, and the logo made it seem as though it might hold something a little fancier. There was only one, and my size was stamped on the side.

They were Tacks 452s. Tacks was a name I remembered from my one winter of hockey all those years ago, and I remembered it as the brand whose name was spoken in hushed tones. They were beautiful skates.

I tried them on and knew right away they would work. Compared to the boxy fit of my old tube skates, these were the highest of high tech. The arch support fit like a new pair of socks, I could feel the stability in the blade, and I even rocked forward and back a bit, my weight thrown comfortably forward by the space-age boots. I was sold.

The price tag said $245, but they cost under two hundred. The cashier didn't have any explanation for this, but I think it was store policy to unload whatever they could to make room for the camping gear. It was like buying bagged-up donuts late in the day.

The next Friday I was back at Leaside Arena, ten minutes before noon, in one of the dressing rooms where

I'd tied Wesley's skates so many times, struggling to get my gear on while trying to avoid looking like I didn't know what I was doing. I doubt I was fooling anyone. I was last on the ice by a good five minutes, and when my chance came I rushed out, my new skates fleet beneath my feet.

The game was fast, but when the puck came my way early on, I was ready and put my new skates to work.

When I got off the ice two minutes later, I couldn't believe how tired I was. My throat was parched and my head was soaked. The equipment was heavy and hot and awkward. My legs felt like they were made of cheese.

I gasped for air on the bench and reached for a water bottle, only to remember I hadn't brought one. I stole a squirt from someone else's, taking as little as I possibly could. Then it was time to go out again.

By my third or fourth shift I was beginning to feel slightly less useless, but still had no speed or agility. I also saw that I was very unlikely to contribute anything at all, and would do best just to stay out of the way.

Even that proved difficult. I was playing defence when the other team's centre picked up a loose puck and hammered a shot from just inside the blue line. I saw my chance to do something and stayed where I was to block it. The puck caught my left knee, just on the inside, in a little gap between the padded areas, one of the few places the front of my body wasn't covered in armour.

I made a sound that surprised my ears, pain shot through my leg, and I fell to the ice like a ton of bricks. I felt like my leg had been cut off at the knee. It took a good minute before I could put enough weight on the thing to get on my feet and wobble to the bench.

I'd seen the guy who had shot the puck come in to get dressed, and he'd clearly come from an office job where going to the water cooler qualified as exercise. Yet this dumpy, middle-aged grey-flannel suit had been able to spin my kneecap like a pinwheel with a slightly hard wrist shot.

I waited out three more shifts until the throbbing began to subside, and even then I could barely skate, but I made myself do it for the sake of pride, such as it was.

When I got home, I had a maroon patch on my knee the size of a saucer. Every time I felt it, I thought of those NHL defencemen who actually choose to get in front of a slap shot taken by someone like Al McInnis, putting himself in the path of a ninety-eight-mile-an-hour cannon without a second thought.

I also thought of the ten-year-old players I had been sending out into battle all winter long.

* * *

When it came to Wesley, hockey and danger hadn't really intersected in my mind before this year. He wasn't very big when he started, and all of that padding seemed even thicker piled onto such a small frame. Even when he crashed into another player, neither was very heavy, nor did they have very far to fall.

The size of the players wasn't really cause for alarm this year, either. Some of the boys, by the end of the season, had begun their pre-adolescent spurt, the one that begins with the feet and works its way up from there, but it wasn't enough to make them any more of a threat on the ice. Most of the time the bigger kids were just figuring out how to move with their newly lengthened limbs.

Their shots weren't much of a threat, either. It would hurt to get hit with one, but there was no comparison between any of their shots and that of a grown man.

The one factor that was a little alarming, though, was their speed.

Humans, it seems, always learn speed before restraint. It's true for toddlers. It's true for scientists. It's true for ten-year-olds playing hockey.

Speed arrived sometime between November and February this past year. Just like the growth spurts they'd go through, it started with the feet. Bigger feet meant more skate blade underneath. They may not always have been able to concentrate long enough to understand the drill we were asking them to do, or to understand where they were supposed to be on the ice at any given time, or even remember where they left their jockstrap after practice, but every one of the boys on the select team could focus on a target at the other end of the rink and put everything they had into getting there first.

By the end of February they were getting there very, very quickly.

A hockey skate takes all of a person's weight and places it on two very narrow blades that slide on a surface with almost no friction. On top of that, the edges of those blades are sharp enough to dig in to the ice. Add in the base level of energy put out by a ten-year-old child, and you've got tremendous potential.

The other factor is the way the skate blade is cut.

I spoke to the Skate Man at Just Hockey about this.

"How much blade is on the ice at any time?" I asked.

"Very little," he said. "Maybe a quarter inch at most."

So Wesley, at about five feet tall and weighing eighty pounds, can hit great speeds while sliding on a finely cut piece of steel a quarter inch long. He's doing that with nine other kids his size, all doing the same thing, all packed into a contained area with very hard boards on all sides and a frictionless surface below, and they are all chasing after one small piece of hard, black rubber.

Oh, and not one of them knows the meaning of the word "restraint."

Or, if they do, we, the coaches, are trying to teach them to forget it. That's the thing about this game. Restraint is generally a disadvantage. There are times when having the wisdom to think a little longer gives a player an advantage, but the game ten-year-olds play, not surprisingly, tends to go the other way. At ten, a player who hesitates may not be lost, but he or she will probably be chasing someone who didn't.

So, we teach them to do what they already know how to do best: charge, attack, go, dig, sprint, forget what it may cost and get there.

We tell them to keep their heads up, it's true, and never to go into the boards at a right angle, and to stay away from that danger zone three feet out, where, should they be hit, they'd go careening headfirst into the boards. But most of these lessons take a while to sink in, and with that last one you don't get many chances.

Every once in a while the father in me wonders just what it is that I am asking my only son to do.

In those times, though, I have to remind myself that I am not, in fact, asking him to do anything. He is asking *me* if he can do it. And it seems that, no matter how much of it he does, it is never, ever enough.

Bodychecking is not allowed in Wesley's age group, although "contact" is. It is a fine distinction. "Contact" means the players can jostle each other for the puck, but they can't skate at full speed and crash into the player to get him off the puck.

Starting next year, however, they can.

Checking in minor hockey is always an issue, but it's become more of one lately. In 2002, the Canadian Hockey Association announced a rule change. Instead of introducing checking at the minor pee wee level, the year players turn eleven, they dropped the age to the minor atom level, the year players turn nine.

The decision was based on a study that had been running since 1998, where competitive teams (select and above) in Ontario and Saskatchewan had lowered the checking age and measured what happened.

The study showed no increase in injuries among the

nine- and ten-year-olds who had been checking compared to those who weren't.

So, the CHA decided to approve checking at the younger age across the country, and at all levels. They reasoned that kids need to learn how to play safely with body contact. Kids generally learn by trial and error. If they start learning before they have started their adolescent growth spurt, the errors might be less costly.

The motion was carried at the CHA's 2002 annual general meeting in Toronto. They also approved a new penalty that carries a one-game suspension: checking to the head. It's an attempt, the press release tells us, to address the increasingly serious number of concussions in hockey.

Both of these changes were unveiled in the same press release.

The irony, apparently, was lost on the CHA, but not on a whole lot of hockey parents.

"Nine-year-olds checking? It's ridiculous."

That's what Monica said when I asked her. She's generally a very gentle, almost shy woman, but her son, Taylor, is one of the biggest kids on the select team, and her husband, Brad, is the team trainer.

"When Brad took the trainer course at Hockey Canada he learned right off that the greatest number of injuries come when the players are twelve and thirteen years old. That's when they introduce checking, and it's an age when their bodies are changing very suddenly and they may not be able to control their playing safely. They're also learning to manage their emotions. There aren't many sports where that kind of behaviour is permitted, let alone encouraged. Football and rugby, maybe . . . but those games aren't generally introduced until the kids are in high school.

"There's a bit of hero worship around players who can really hit. There's a fine line there. They're supposed to check, but if they hurt another player, they get thrown out of the game, sometimes suspended, and players *do* get hurt. There are people crumpled on the ice at every game, as it is. There haven't been any serious injuries yet, but there have been hits to the head and the potential is only going to go up.

"One thing seems fairly clear to me: at the select level, and even in A, these kids aren't going to the NHL. Maybe at the AAA level, but what good is a checking game doing for everyone else? It seems like a very traditional kind of hierarchy is making these decisions, as if the way things have been done in the past is more important than the way things are happening now. After the Salt Lake City Olympics last year, everyone from the sportswriters to the hockey parents said it was the best hockey they'd ever seen—and there was almost no emphasis on the physical game. Why would anyone want to move away from that?"

• • •

When I was the age Wesley is now, I played football. I watched the Canadian Football League on TV with my dad and I knew how the game worked. I knew I'd be driving myself headfirst into other players. That's what I wanted.

I was a big kid who was scared to push back. Kids smell that kind of thing, and there were two short kids in my grade who went to town on it. As I remember it, they bugged me every day after school, waiting at the edge of the park I crossed to get home. But, all these decades later, it's hard to be sure. It may have been that they bugged me a little and I thought about it all the time. Either way, by the sixth grade I was tired of it and wanted to learn to be tough, so I joined the football team at Patricia Park.

After the second or third practice, Harry, the head coach, took me aside. He walked me to the end of the field and told me to get into a three-point stance— crouched, with both feet on the end zone line, and one fist planted on the ground in front of me.

"When I blow the whistle," he said, "I want you to dive."

"Dive?" I asked.

"Dive. Just launch yourself forward and land on your chest."

I tried, but it came out more like a half-hearted jump. I landed on my feet and rolled forward onto my chest.

"Was that a dive?" he asked.

I said no, it wasn't.

"Why didn't you dive?"

I couldn't answer.

"I'll tell you why," he said. "You're scared. When you were a baby, learning to walk, you did this all the time. Look how much padding you've got on. Is it really going to hurt?"

I didn't say anything, but I was pretty sure it would. I couldn't actually see myself doing it.

"Ready?" he asked, and he blew the whistle again.

I tried again, this time pushing off with more strength. My feet tried to come up and land for me again, but I'd committed myself too far. I landed on my chest, felt the air rush out of me and heard a dull thud echoing inside my helmet.

"You hurt?" he asked.

I waited a second and realized I wasn't.

"Do it again."

I was more confident this time, and I made a deeper thud when I landed. I got up and the coach blew the whistle again. And again. And again. And again. We stopped when I reached the other goal line. I had turf embedded in my face mask and a rush of adrenaline coursing through my body as if it had been waiting there my whole life.

It was slightly different in a game, but the equation was really the same. On offence, I was a lineman. Every time we got the ball, the play started with me face to face with, and one step away from, another player. My job was to plough into him with all my strength and push him out of the play, to throw myself at him with complete abandon. The real game was learning to overcome my fear; succeeding at that was just as intoxicating as that very first time. If I failed because he anticipated my move, or somehow outsmarted me, then I would come back the next time with more intensity. But if I failed because I got scared and hesitated, I would spend the rest of the game waiting for it to happen again, and again and again.

There was a big linebacker on the Hampstead team. We named him Gronk because he reminded us of some sort of primitive man—a wealthy, loud-mouthed, private-schooled caveman. He not only terrorized us, but he gloated. He would penetrate our offensive line, throw our quarterback to the ground, and roar like a bull who has gored the matador.

I remember the anger rising up within me with every play. I had been frustrated before in games and felt my neck tightening and teeth involuntarily grinding, but this was different. I started charging at him every play, whether it made sense in our strategy or not, pounding at him until he had to take notice. It was the same kind of decision as diving into the turf for a hundred and ten yards at a time. I was scared, but my anger took over. Anger was the protecting force, the reinforcements summoned when all hope was lost.

We eventually beat that Hampstead team—and Gronk—and our team's confidence soared. We were all at the dawn of adolescence and thrilled at the power we had discovered. We walked taller and bellowed in the dressing room after games. It was new and thrilling. We were invincible.

In the last game before the playoffs, while we were defending deep in our end, the opposing quarterback stepped back to pass, just as one of our bigger linemen broke through and caught him by surprise. I don't remember our lineman's name, but he was a tall kid—and fast. In three powerful steps, without slowing at all, he lowered his head and drove all of his weight, helmet first, right into the quarterback's stomach. The poor kid was standing flat-footed and didn't stand a chance. He folded like an empty bag and his coaches had to carry him off.

I can still hear the sound of that collision, a sickening mix of the crack of the helmet and the soft crumpling of the other player. I doubt our lineman has forgotten it, either. He stood, bewildered, trying to understand what he'd done.

The next season I changed teams and leagues and ended up playing beside Gronk. He was a friendly kid, I found, whose feelings were often hurt by things the other guys said in the dressing room. His real name was Myron.

*　*　*

May drags on. Soccer hasn't started yet. Wesley's funk deepens.

One afternoon, on a neighbourhood walk, we bump into Roman. He and I talk about the season, how well things had gone for a team so full of first-timers, and contentedly deem ourselves and our children successes all around.

Back at the apartment, Wesley is livid.

"What about me?" he bursts out. "No one's asking *me* how I feel about losing the season. No one's asking *me* about that, about hockey stopping like that with no warning. You guys talk about it like it doesn't matter, like we don't need it."

I am taken aback, but I try to follow the advice I've read in the parenting books—identify feelings and reflect them back.

"You're feeling angry," I say—which, when taken out of context, seems something the far side of lame, but it is, if nothing else, accurate.

"Yes, I'm angry," he fumes. "Before I had somewhere to put it. That's how I stopped that guy on the Downsview team. That's how I stole the puck and scored that goal. I was angry and I used it. Now, I can't."

He storms out. I am left in the kitchen, wondering about anger and hockey, and which one was protecting us from the other. An image that had been troubling me comes back to mind: my son's joyous love of the game locked away behind a flimsy set of doors, with a stolen car, the engine racing, pointed dead ahead, waiting for something to throw it in gear.

# VII

IT'S THE LAST WEEK OF SUMMER, a week before Labour Day. Wesley and I are driving north from Toronto to the little town of South River, Ontario, which is only south if you're in North Bay.

Sometime during the winter I agreed to help organize the hockey camp this summer. Until now, that meant keeping track of how many campers were involved and sending out emails that explained what to bring and where to go. But today it means *showing* them where to go, which is an entirely different thing. The arena in South River, where we are all meeting and where the campers will play every day, is a twenty-minute, twisting, baffling, mostly unmarked drive through cottage-road oblivion.

Derek is riding north with us. Guy, his father, asked if I could take him along, and to make sure he's settled when we get there. This will be Derek's first trip away from his family. Guy suspected he might be feeling nervous and wanted to make sure he is comfortable.

Derek is eleven now, as Wesley will be in another few months. They are in the back seat, talking as if I'm not here. While I think about how I might make sure these young boys feel safe at night, they are discussing foul language in popular music, graphic violence in computer games, and what it will feel like to flatten other players on the hockey rink.

They are just weeks away from the beginning of their minor pee wee year of hockey, when, at the select level, bodychecking is introduced. It's all any of the players have been talking about.

• • •

It is midafternoon. Outside the leaves are at the final edge of summer greenery. The breeze is gentle. The sun is hot. The younger group of players has already finished its first skating session and is heading off to camp, armed with my cobbled-together directions and following, one car after another, in a caravan of rising dust.

Inside the arena, Wesley and I are gliding through the haze as if we never left: the cool, nitrous smell of the ice, the dull thud of the puck on the boards, the pervading half-light that floats at eye level—nothing has changed.

It is a strange irony that this country, yearly tossed between choking heat and lethal cold, blazing sun and impenetrable dark, with a people who look to the whim of the land to tell them who they are, has embraced a game largely played in a featureless, permanent grey that is exactly the same anywhere in the country at any time of year.

Clearly, if this is something to complain about, it is lost on me—and on my son. We are thrilled. I feel the rush of the air around me again and I want only to skate. We charge up and down the ice, weaving between the other players, a puck sliding between us. For a few minutes I am back in Leaside Arena on those early Saturday mornings years ago, when it is just the two of us—a father who hasn't yet learned what he lacks, and a son who hasn't learned to notice. He turns up ice again. I send him a puck and chase, but a whistle blast fills the air and the moment is gone.

It is the camp's volunteer head coach, Mike, starting the practice.

The players are agitated and slow to gather round, talking and pushing in a clump. Mike puts the whistle to his lips to blow it again when a small player skates forward with a question. Mike has to bend down to hear him. The boy is slim and fragile.

"When do we start checking?" he asks.

Silence fills the rink as the others stare, waiting for the answer.

. . .

The camp's adult volunteers get together that night.

We have a great set-up. We live in a clutch of cabins up the hill from the north end of the beach. I have chosen the central cabin with an open main room that acts as our clubhouse for evening gatherings. My room is in the back. The bed is, as in every cabin, a narrow bunk built of unfinished pine two-by-fours with a foam mattress. There is a set of shelves and a window.

The camp owner had a fridge installed in the main room before we arrived, and thanks to at least a few well-prepared souls, it is already lined with beer.

The first to arrive is Peter Shier. He will be Mike's assistant coach for the week. We sit down to a beer together and I learn very quickly that Peter is a real hockey player.

He is from Montreal, but went to school in the States —at Cornell, in Ithaca, New York. He starred on their varsity team, was named an All-American and set a string of school scoring records.

"I played from the time I was four or five, but I never thought about it as a career," he says. "Then I got calls from the New York Rangers and the Minnesota North Stars. It was kind of a surprise.

"I went with the North Stars because they were the worst team and I figured I'd have a better chance of getting on; but then, about a week before training camp, they merged with another NHL team that was folding— the Cleveland Barons. There were 150 guys at camp. So I ended up on the North Stars' Central League farm team in Oklahoma City.

"Remember *Slap Shot,* the movie? Well, that was basically our team. We had games in Tulsa and Birmingham that turned into wars—fighting in the stands, police escorts to get out of there. It was kind of surreal, really. When I read clippings from that time and remember what we did, it's just unbelievable."

The others have come in. Chris, Anne, Lorraine, Leanne and Neil, parents of Wesley's teammates Andrew, Shawn, Graeme, Alex and Douglas, respectively. The last to come in is Mike Harvey, the coach.

"I spent three years at Cornell and there were no fights," Peter says. "None. It was [punishable by a] three-game suspension and that was a third of the season. Nobody did it."

"My dad always told us not to fight," Mike says. "He was my coach for all those years. 'Don't fight,' he said. 'Fighting is wrong. It's stupid and pointless and there are always better ways to settle things. If you fight, you get kicked out of the game, and you don't get to play anymore and you might even get hurt. Don't fight.'

"Then he waited a second, looking away, before he turned back.

"'Now,' my dad said, 'when you get in your first fight . . .'" and Mike pauses for the laugh.

"'When you get in your first fight,' he said to us, 'don't stop hitting. The ref is going to tell you to stop, but if *you* do and the other guy doesn't, then you get the shit beat out of you. You're getting kicked out of the game either way. There's no point in getting kicked out of a game *and* getting beaten up, so don't stop hitting.'"

"And?" Neil asks.

"Well, there was this guy hacking at our goalie. He was really at him and the ref wasn't calling anything. I came off of my shift and my dad said, 'Look, you've got to stand up for your goalie. You've *got* to.'

"'But,' I said, and he just looked at me.

"So the next time that guy hacked at our goalie and I was on the ice, I pushed him away, hard. There was a second when we looked at each other, and then I thought, 'Here we go,' and I dropped my gloves and started hitting him."

"Then the ref told you both to stop," Peter says.

"Right," Mike says. "And the other guy *did* stop hitting." He smiles.

"Dad was right." And the room explodes in laughter.

I tell a story about driving Wesley and Melissa somewhere recently. We were verging on late. The traffic was bad. They had been bickering back home, and now things were escalating. The final straw came when I heard a smack and Melissa cried out. I pulled the car over and let Wesley have it.

"You *can't* do that! You can't!" I said. "I don't care what she did, when you hit her, you've gone too far. If you did that in hockey," I shout, "you'd be kicked out of the game!"

"If you yelled like that while you were coaching," Wesley said, his eyes narrowed, "you'd be kicked out, too."

This earns a few appreciative nods.

"That sure wasn't true in Oklahoma." Peter says. "It took a lot to get kicked out of those games."

I ask him what it was like to work so hard for something for so many years, and have it turn out so unlike what he'd dreamt.

"Well, I never really did dream of it," Peter says. "I just liked to play hockey and I followed where it took me.

"When I was a kid, one of my neighbours played with the Bruins—Dave Forbes. He gave me a great piece of advice. 'If you're going to play professionally,' he said, 'give yourself a time limit. Don't end up hanging around the minors for twenty years waiting for the big break.'

"So I said two years, and after two years I decided to pack it in. But then I heard about guys playing in Europe. I was still in my mid-twenties. I thought, what the hell? I had no idea what to expect.

"I signed with this team in the 'A' League in Finland, in a little blue-collar town called Rauma, three hours outside of Helsinki. It was instant independence and very lonely. I mean, I'd been away from home when I was at school, but everything was still in English at Cornell. There was really no English in Rauma at all—no papers, no radio . . . just *The Muppet Show* on TV once a week with Finnish subtitles.

"But the hockey was the best I've ever played. Really. It was just before European players started moving to the NHL in real numbers. Jari Kurri was playing, and there were so many others at that level—incredible talents, and *fast*. The ice surface was huge. It was like playing pond hockey with 10,000 people watching, and there was no garbage, no fighting at all. None.

"I was always curious about what they were saying in papers about us after the game, whether they thought I was playing well or not, but there were only a couple of guys on the team who could speak English, and not very well, at that." Peter says. "It was strange to be in such a fantastic hockey situation and not be able to share it with anyone."

The party broke up late that night. I turned in to the sound of the lake outside my window, and I thought of Wesley and the same sound reaching him on the other side of the camp. I tried to picture him, wondering if he was asleep, and I realized I hadn't seen him after he'd picked out his bunk. I didn't even know which cabin he was in. Then it occurred to me that he didn't know which one I was in, either.

• • •

Something is nagging at my memory about last night's conversation with Peter. He mentioned his neighbour in Montreal, Dave Forbes, who had played for the Bruins.

I hook up my laptop in the camp office, do an Internet search, and there he is.

Dave Forbes is on record, to quote one biographer, as the most "pernicious perpetrator of goonery in an era of acute and brutal violence."

In the 1974–75 season, in January, he jabbed the butt end of his stick directly into the eye of the Minnesota

North Stars' Henry Boucha. Boucha never recovered and was forced to retire. Forbes was suspended for ten games by the NHL, and charged with aggravated assault in Minnesota District Court, but after eighteen hours of deliberation, the jury couldn't reach a verdict, and Forbes played in the NHL for another five years.

By the time Peter Shier was finding the game he'd always dreamt of in Finland, Dave Forbes was retired from hockey and had become an ordained minister in California.

· · ·

The players are lined up along the blue line.

"*Never,*" Mike is saying, in the only kind of voice that really carries in a hockey rink, "never get caught here." And he places himself three feet away from the boards, his back to the group.

"All it will take is a tiny tap," and Peter Shier skates in and makes to push him from behind, "and you're in big trouble." Mike feigns to fall forward, his head arcing menacingly toward the board's hard upper edge.

"Almost worse is doing that to someone else," he goes on. "The boards are your protection if you stay close. You'll get squeezed and maybe fall down, that's all. That's why you wear all that padding. Falling down against the boards won't hurt you. Falling *into* them can break your neck."

The players nod. This is a group of boys that normally has trouble staying still when they sleep, but here they are standing motionless, eyes forward, jaws set.

"One more thing about getting hit," Mike says, and the boys know they're only a few moments away from the thing they've been thinking of for so long. "It's going to scare you. You're going to be skating along with the puck, or looking for a pass to make, and then you're going to look up and see it coming and think, 'Oh, no, I'm going to die.' And then you'll get hit and you'll be flat on your back and someone else will be skating away with the puck and you're going to think you need to be carried out in a coffin.

"That's when you ask yourself, 'Am I dead?' You'll realize you are not. Ask yourself, 'Am I hurt?' The answer is probably 'no.' 'Do I feel stupid?' Well, that's a different story—probably yes. 'Will I be okay?' Yes. 'Should I get up now?' Yes. 'Do I want to keep playing?'

"YES!" the kids all call in response.

"All right, then," Mike says. "Be smart. Use the boards. Keep your head up."

The players nod in unison.

We begin with two players along the boards. One skates in a gentle curve around the corner and behind the net. The other slowly follows after and gradually squeezes the first player into the boards, eventually pinning him there. Everything is in slow motion.

After every player has been through that several times, the speed moves up to a very relaxed pace. The players going in first are not scared. They are not getting hurt. They are not dying.

After a water break, Mike lines them up again. There are twenty-two of them in a line, single file, half a step away from the boards.

"This drill will show you that getting squished into the boards is not going to hurt," Mike says. "You're all going to stand where you are, and the first player in line is going to skate between you and the boards. As he goes by, I want each of you to check him."

The first to go is James, the biggest kid on the select team. He's clearly in control and he only loses his balance when Andrew, who is strong on his skates and has plenty of oomph, lets him have it as he's near the end of the line. Some players cheer, and laugh, but most are focused on the task at hand, and as James takes his place at the end of the line, another starts into the fray.

Wesley is one of the bigger kids. He doesn't hesitate as he goes through the line, but there is a coldness in his eyes that I haven't seen before. This is a job to do and he is determined to do it, pushing past Taylor, grimacing against Andrew and bracing with conviction when James lands into him and he is pinned before driving on through the line.

Half the players have gone through now, and so far none has had any kind of incident. Standing back a bit, though, a profile emerges from the line of players along the boards. Like a city skyline, there are big ones, tall ones, wide ones, and some that, by comparison, are not very big at all. Wesley's linemate, Nathan, is one of those, and right beside him, smaller still, is Derek.

Derek, I can see, is nervously biting his lip, still several spots away from running the gauntlet. He's a brave kid, and always has been, but the idea of putting himself between someone like James and a section of hardened plywood can't be something he's looking forward to.

Mike sees me looking at him and nods. As Derek's turn approaches, Mike skates to the front of the line and stands by his side.

"The job of a check is to push the other player off the puck and to get him out of the play long enough to take possession," Mike says. "That's all a good check has to do. Any more than that and you're taking chances—sometimes big chances. If the other player turns his back to you just before you hit him, it's your fault. Even if you barely make contact, a hit from behind is a game misconduct and a one-game suspension, as well. You'll be sent home for that game and the next. And if you really hit someone from behind, you could paralyze him, and then you've got no one to blame but yourself.

"A hit to the head of any kind is the same." And he looks directly at James, Wesley and Taylor, the tall section of this team's skyline. "Even if a player only comes up to your chest, if you hit his head, it's your fault. These are choices that you have to make. You have to live with the consequences of what you do. Think.

"Now," and he looks down at Derek, "these guys are all bigger than you, but you're just as tough as any of them. I'm not going to tell them to go easy on you because no other team is going to do that, and that's not what this is about. It's about learning to safely absorb a check. You can do that. I know it, and everyone else here knows it, too."

Then Mike whispers something to Derek through a cupped hand. Derek takes a breath and charges ahead.

Wesley holds back when he checks Derek—I see him decide to do that. Andrew does a bit, too. But James lines him up and crunches him like a candy wrapper. Derek's feet swoop out from under him and he tumbles onto his side on the ice. There is a silence while James looks down at him, a look of concern on his face. Derek scrambles to his feet, crouches down a bit and launches himself up and into the next player with such force that the other guy spills to the ice in a spray of feet and gloves.

Derek catches Mike's eye and gives a little grin.

"Lower centre of gravity," Mike says to me out of the corner of his mouth. "That's what I told him to do. Works every time."

• • •

The week is spectacular—glorious sunshine every day, cool and clear every night. It's a week of gentle aimlessness where the minutes crawl by and days are over in a breath.

On the last night of camp we hold a skills competition and scrimmage, and near the end of the night there is a wonderful moment. Mike and Peter have joined the game, one on either team. Mike plays defence, and Peter is on the wing. Wesley is on Peter's team, and when his line goes on I see what it is that I wish I could do.

Wesley's strength as a player is his ability to see the play as it might unfold and react to it. With Peter on his wing, in just a few seconds it's clear that instead of anticipating the way things are going, Wesley is simply part of something that is unfolding all around him. He can go freely through the spaces he sees, knowing the puck is on its way to him, even before he can think about it. It is a delightful thing to see. He moves through a crowd at the top of the face-off circle, Peter sends the puck, and in that instant the jumble of players becomes an ordered swirl around something that seems to have been inevitable all along—Wesley receiving the puck and streaming toward the net.

I watch this happen again and again, and when Wesley comes off the ice he wears a grin I recognize instantly. It is the face of play, the face of a boy having too much fun to even know how wonderful that is.

We have a party that night around a bonfire back at camp.

I thank Mike and Peter for all they've done, and hours later, when the beer is all gone and the kids all asleep, I wobble back to my bed, dreaming of making the pass— feeling the impulse, seeing the path, sending the puck and feeling it land—a moment of connection between us, one supporting the other, and simultaneously sending him out into the game, ready to act on his own.

2003–2004

**LEASIDE 2003–04 MINOR PEEWEE SELECT FLAMES**
*Front:* Taylor Martin, Ryan Malion, Devin Montrose, Derek
Perry, Harrison Levy, Nathan Robbins-Kanter, Chris Fallis,
Patrick Maulson, Devlin Brand.
*Middle:* Ben Sankey, Evan Blair, Alex Small, Reed Picton, Wesley
Allen, James Bolt, Robert Zend-Gabori, Aidan Totten, Andrew
Kowalczyszyn, Jonathan Hart, Charlie Casper.
*Back:* Andrew Bolt, Brad Martin, Dave Picton, Roman
Kowalczyszyn.
*Missing:* Me.

# VIII

DAVE, ROMAN, BRAD AND I are leaving a sports bar in late September and walking into the cool evening air. We have just enjoyed a beer together for the first time in months, but none of us is feeling particularly relaxed.

Once again, we will be coaching the select team this season. Dave is the head coach, Roman and I are assistants. Brad is the trainer. We drove here directly from the rink about an hour ago, after ninety minutes of skating at New Centre Ice. It was the final tryout for this year's team.

Twenty-six boys tried out. Fifteen will make the team. We are phoning the others tonight.

Last year there were only three who tried and didn't make it, and in each case their skills were so noticeably below the others that their parents, who'd watched the try-outs, suspected as much and prepared them for the worst.

Still, the calls weren't easy. This year they're going to be brutal.

Three talented new players arrived at the tryouts: one down from the "A" team, another up from a lower age group, another new to the neighbourhood. Yet another turned up just playing a whole lot better than he did last year.

We could see it in the first minutes of the first skate. Several of the boys who were part of last year's team wouldn't be on this one.

For many, ours was the first team they'd belonged to. We spent last year building a sense of trust and respect between players. Being on the team meant no one would unfairly criticize your play. The coaches would be honest and positive. The team supported the players when things were bad and celebrated with them when things were good. Players learned together and played together and knew that the others would defend them when they needed it. The team was a safe place.

Now, some of those boys will be cut.

This year we've decided on an early-morning week-day practice with a professional skating coach in addition to the usual ninety minutes on Saturday mornings. There is also a select game and a house-league game. That will add up to more than three hours of skating every week.

The players we're phoning tonight will only play one house-league game per week, giving them only about fif-teen minutes of ice time. They'll be watching the select players skate circles around them, and those circles will get faster every week.

We've tried to soften some of that by naming an alternate list—three players who will come to all the practices but will only play in games when one of the regulars can't make it. It's going to be cold comfort, though. Two of those three alternates were members of last year's team, and one is Wesley's favourite linemate, Nathan.

The goalie situation is also tense. Matti won a spot on the "A" team this year, but Patrick is returning. That leaves only one spot for three others, all of whom are strong candidates. Of those, two are new prospects; the third tried out last year and was cut, even after his mother informed us that he'd been told if he made the team he'd get a brand new set of goalie equipment for Christmas.

He got the equipment anyway.

Still, cutting him a second time was going to be tough, so we have decided to take on three goalies. Patrick will play half of every game, while the other two will share the remaining time. We've invited the fourth to the goalie training sessions we'll be having early mornings.

I have two calls to make tonight. One is to Graeme, a very determined defenceman who has tried out before, but whose skating has set him behind.

His mother, Lorraine, answers the phone. She came along when Graeme attended hockey camp this year. He worked hard and improved a great deal in that week, but it wasn't enough. I tell Lorraine I'm calling for Graeme, and I hear in her silence a dread I know too well. She asks me to hold on. I hear her call his name, and I have a few more seconds to collect my words.

The irony settles in as I wait. I am telling this boy, who skates more or less like I do, that he is not good enough and therefore will not be allowed to come to our practices, to play in our games, to learn from our coaches or become part of our community.

Graeme is not happy. He asks why he's been cut. He asks for specifics, and all I can tell him is that his skating needs more work and to keep playing every chance he gets. I tell him how impressed we were with his improvements at the hockey camp. I tell him how we admired his work ethic and his commitment—all absolutely true, but my words sound false. I am full of praise, but that is not why I have called, and we both know that. I finally end the conversation, but with no resolution from Graeme. He is still not satisfied, and there is nothing I can do about that.

This year's toughest call came early. Dave made it after the second tryout. The player had been on last year's team. He is a good skater; he is bright and has a quick sense of humour and the other boys like him. His mother worked hours and hours for the team last year as our business manager and helped to organize the hockey camp that helped so many of the players who are coming back. The player we cut is Shawn, Anne's son.

Shawn is in a gifted program at school. Many times he saw patterns emerging and reacted to them quickly, but that meant leaving his position. He saw he was needed somewhere else, and he went.

The coach's job is to bring some order to the game by eliminating variables. There are always going to be surprises, good and bad, but if some parameters are set and reliable—if the right winger is always on the right side of the ice, for example—the others on the team can build on that, making more and more choices, taking control of the game.

In order for that to work, though, the individual players have to give up control. Shawn either didn't want to, or couldn't. Either way, Dave didn't like it.

Rather than wait for an inevitably painful moment, once the coaches saw what was going to happen we decided to be direct and honest and to give Shawn the respect he deserved by telling him early on.

That was a week ago. I still don't know if it was the right thing to do. Several players who were clearly less skilled came for the second and third tryouts, while Shawn simply didn't return. It is too late for him to find another select team this year, and for the rest of the season he and every one else he sees at house-league games will know that of all the players who tried out, he was cut first.

"Shawn is very, very angry," Anne told me when I went by the house this week. "*I'm* angry. I'm angry at Dave. He never liked Shawn, and Shawn knew it. I guess I thought that maybe because I'd been manager it might have changed something, even though I wouldn't want Shawn to make the team for that reason, but it's very confusing.

"All you really want is for your kid to be able to achieve something on their own. He loves hockey and he's very determined, but this hasn't been a good experience. All last year, coming home from games, he was upset. He knew it wasn't good. Dave didn't have to say anything, and I don't even think Dave did. Shawn just knew.

"We could see he was out of position, but what could we do? Shawn saw things he thought were important and he acted on his convictions. That's not a bad characteristic for a kid, but in hockey, it's been a fault.

"He'll come around, but he's still very hurt—especially knowing he was one of the first cut. He came home, took his hockey gear out of the bag that says 'Leaside' on the side and gave the bag to Ryan, his little brother, along with his Leaside jacket and his Leaside toque. He said he refused to advertise for Leaside for as long as he lives."

I still have bad feelings towards the coach who cut Wesley two years ago. I see him now and then and, in the same way it was for Wesley, a good part of me is still waiting for something—an apology, an admission, I don't know . . . something to address a decision that had such an impact on my son's life.

I can't help but wonder how many of the parents I see around the arena are thinking the same thing now.

My one protection is that there is truly no doubt about Wesley deserving to be on this team, which isn't always the case. There are always stories, especially at the higher levels of kids' hockey, about players who got on the team because Dad is a coach, or a friend of the coach, or bought new skates for everyone—or, believe it or not, because Mom is a babe.

Wesley doesn't have to worry about any suggestions of favouritism. Most people, if they see us on the ice together, have trouble believing we come from the same gene pool.

Wesley was shocked when we cut Shawn. It immediately drew a cold and hard line between friends and colleagues. The hardest cut for Wesley, though, is finding out that Nathan is on the alternate list.

"How could you do that?" he asks me in disbelief. "He skates, he shoots, he passes, he scores. What else does he have to do?"

My answer doesn't help him at all. Nathan is courageous and hard-working and generous. He is quick and smart and honest and easy to get along with. These are the qualities that schools, religious institutions and community organizations consider the foundation for a successful life. If a person has these qualities, we have been teaching our children every day of their lives, they will be fulfilled.

But in the national game, none of that matters if some mouth-breathing dolt on the other team can push you off the puck because he's twice your size.

Checking starts this year. Nathan is not very big, and that will make it harder for him to stay on the puck, to dig it out of the corners, to bounce back when he's taken into the boards. It doesn't mean he won't be able to do those things; he just might not be able to do them quite as well as somebody bigger. In the end, there was only one spot open for two small players. One was Derek and the other was Nathan. Dave has always liked Derek's sense of where to be and, as Dave put it, his "nose for the goal." Dave wasn't certain Nathan would be quite as effective, and in a close tryout, that's all it takes: a reasonable doubt.

The parking lot is just as dingy as ever at New Centre Ice when I pull in for the team's first practice. The dumpster from the Chinese buffet smells the same. The downstairs bar is still under renovation. The paint in the lobby is still grey and cracked, and the video games send out the same screams, even though there is still no one there. But as the team warms up on the ice and lines up along the blue line to begin a new season, something is decidedly different. Everyone belongs here, but three players don't belong quite as much as the others, anymore

. . .

I did something impulsive after the select practice today.

There was a table set up in the lobby, beside the video games. A guy in his thirties was sitting behind it, forms and pens laid out before him. He had a sign mounted on the wall behind him that read "Toronto Ice Hockey League."

"We're here weeknights and weekends," the guy said. He was birdlike, and slightly earnest. "It's all non-contact.

Three hundred fifty bucks for the season—twenty-six games, plus playoffs."

"Um," I said.

I looked at the forms.

He looked at me again.

"We have all levels," he said.

We looked at each other some more, and then, still surprising myself, I said, "Okay. What do I do?"

"Sign here and here," he said. "This is a waiver. You've already missed this week's game, but we can find a place for you in time for next week. What level do you play?"

"What levels are there?"

"A through D."

"D," I said, very quickly.

I wrote the cheque. Wesley wasn't finished getting changed yet. I waited in the lobby as kids and parents came and went.

Two men came up to the table. They were carrying hockey sticks and giant equipment bags that they dropped with thuds to the floor. The guy behind the table apparently knew them, because he didn't have to explain anything. They grunted hello, signed the forms and handed him cheques, then swung their bags back up on their shoulders and lumbered away.

They were huge—really big lads, with voices that rumbled like truck traffic and hair sprouting out all over the place. I watched them walk away. They couldn't fit through the corridor side by side.

"Dad . . ." came a push from my side. Wesley was looking at me. He was ready to go and had his stuff packed in
his bag. It seemed like he'd been there a while.

"What is it?" he asked.

"Huh?" I said, still watching the two behemoths,
wondering if I'd lost my mind.

• • •

I *had* lost my mind.

I am once again at New Centre Ice, in the same dressing rooms where, every Saturday morning, I tighten
Wesley's skates and, ninety minutes later, duck while the
snowball wars rage between the boys. Except it isn't a
Saturday morning—it is Sunday night—and I am tying
my own skates in a room full of grown men doing the
same, and we are all pulling on our team jerseys.

The jerseys don't say much across the front—just
"Toronto Ice Hockey League" around the league logo of
a pair of skates—and, like everything else in this rink,
they are grey.

I'm number 64. There's no significance to that. It's
just the jersey I pulled out of the garbage bag that lay
dumped on the floor when I arrived. But as I look
around, I have to wonder. The other players all have
numbers in the single digits and teens, and they all look
quite a bit younger than me.

I feel the urge to stand up and issue some kind of disclaimer about how I'm just learning to play, that they

shouldn't expect too much, but that doesn't seem like the best way to start.

An email arrived three days ago from the league. It welcomed me, told me when my first game was, and told me the name of my team: the Vultures.

One player, a very tall guy with a big voice, is telling a golf story to another, who is laughing. Studiously not listening is the goalie, who is suited up and looking at a space on the floor just ahead of his feet. He is rocking slightly, breathing through his nose and not speaking.

Two other players stand up and begin to pull on their helmets.

"So," one says. "What have we got?" and answers dribble in.

"I'll play D."

"Wing."

"Me, too."

"I could play centre," the second guy standing says.

"Okay."

A small, slim fellow enters. He's wearing street clothes and carrying an equipment bag. He moves efficiently, and within seconds he is pulling on his gear.

I was here half an hour early, and I've only just finished dressing now.

"What do you play?" one of the guys standing in the middle asks the one who's just swept in.

"I don't care," he mumbles, still moving constantly. "I'll play anywhere."

"Centre?"

"Sure."

"Okay, that's me and Don and . . . ?" He looks at the slim guy.

"Cliff."

"Cliff. Right. We'll play centre. You four can be D, and that leaves wingers. Does that work out?"

"Yup," someone answers. "Six of us."

"Three full lines. Okay—wingers, pair up." And the two leaders, which is clearly what they've become, leave for the ice.

The slim guy, unbelievably, is almost finished dressing. Others are going out, too.

"Right or left?" the guy beside me asks.

"Right, I guess."

"Cool," he says, and walks out.

I'm on my own, in my gear, holding that still brand new "Featherlite" stick. I still don't feel like a hockey player, but it's too late now.

* * *

The puck goes into the corner and I go after it. My legs are wiped, but adrenaline must be kicking in because I still have some energy. A big centre from the other team comes in from the other direction, but I'm already there and I do what I've learned to do—I dig.

Incredibly, it works. I come out the other side with the puck on my stick and the centre turned around behind me. I see the puck there, on my blade. I have control of it.

I am standing by the boards in my team's end—with the puck. I have coached wingers on the select team dozens of times on this very moment. Thoughts rip through my mind. I see Dave's face, the kids on the team, Wesley calling for the puck, sounds, images, words bombarding me by the billions. I still haven't moved, but a voice inside my head louder than all the others screams "PASS!" So I do, to no one, and the puck sails all the way down the ice to the other end. The ref calls icing, brings it back more or less where it was, and I skate to the bench.

My left winger is there ahead of me. I flop beside him on the bench.

"Jesus," he says, huffing.

"Yeah," I say.

That's our conversation.

It's the second period and we're losing 3–1. I am already exhausted, but it really hasn't gone so badly. There are great blocks of time when I feel absolutely useless, but at least I know what's going on in the game. I *understand* my uselessness. And, when it comes to digging along the boards, I'm getting somewhere and can now even get the puck.

I just don't seem to be able to do anything with it.

Most of the time, I panic. That has meant a bunch of bad passes, either into the corner or onto the other team's sticks. But Dave's lessons to the select team have made *some* impression on me, because when one of my teammates gets the puck, I am almost instinctively charging down my side, looking for a pass. It's what a winger does on offence.

And it works. Three times tonight, I have charged down the boards and the puck has come my way—right onto my stick—before it bounced right off again, got lost in my feet or just seemed to be going faster than me.

I remember reading a magazine article about the big power forward for the Vancouver Canucks, Todd Bertuzzi. "He's the man with the hardest hits and softest hands," his agent was quoted as saying, and the phrase stays with me now.

"Soft hands" is such a great expression. It sounds exactly like it looks. You can picture the puck staying right on the player's stick, gently cradled like some delicate treasure, smooth, fast and in control. That's what I want.

It's not what I've got. My hands are hard, they're brittle and clumsy—grasping too hard, swiping at the air in dull, empty arcs, gripping my stick the way an old man clutches his cane while the puck drifts mockingly by.

I need soft hands.

The score stays 3–1. The Vultures lose.

Cliff is undressed and gone before I have my skates off. The rest are in various stages of deconstruction.

I feel guilty that I wasn't able to do more. I could feel the impulses and see the patterns, but my legs wouldn't get me there and my hands never made it worth their while.

"Well, that's better than last week, boys," one of the leaders says.

The room grunts in response. Gear is being pulled off

and tossed into bags, tape ripped off shins and dropped to the floor.

"What's your name?" a guy to my right asks. He played defence, and he sent me one of my mishandled passes. I tell him, and there is the tiniest silence, a moment of hesitation when it seems the room is listening. It's a social re-creation of my moment along the boards. I've got the puck.

"I really just started playing last year," I say. "I never played as a kid, but my son's really into it now and he's pretty good, too, so I thought I'd improve my game a bit—so I can, you know, hold off being completely irrelevant for a few more years. This was my first game. Man, it's harder than it looks. I'm really thirsty." I grab my water bottle and take an enormous chug.

A few of the others are still looking at me.

The slim guy is leaving.

"Great," the defenceman says as he gets up to go. "See you next week."

• • •

Dave has divided the select practice. He has the forwards in one end, while Roman works with the defence in the other. The forwards are learning what is called a "breakout," when they get possession of the puck in their own end and have a plan to quickly move it out.

It is exactly the situation I was in with the Vultures, but here it is ordered and it works. The winger gets the puck along the boards, passes to the centre moving up the middle, who quickly sends a long pass to the far winger now at centre ice. It is such a simple and obvious system. The puck travels so much faster than any player could. All it takes is two well-placed passes and the game is completely turned around.

"Wingers stay wide," Dave calls to Nathan, who has taken the pass from Wesley at centre and is skating down the far side. "Don't go to the net until you're right across the blue line. Stay wide."

Nathan does, but it is clearly counterintuitive. The wingers, once they get the puck and are entering the other team's zone, want to head straight for the goal.

"Stay wide!" Dave calls again, this time to Derek. "Create space!"

"Create space." The words float around the rink for an instant. It's one of those phrases that seems to really mean something in a visceral sense, the same way "soft hands" does. I can feel it just saying the words out loud: "create space." The jumble of bodies and sticks in front of me takes on a geometrical shape, and a line appears. It's the same magic Peter Shier used at hockey camp when he parted the sea of jerseys to deliver the puck to my son.

I skate off to centre ice, leaving the forwards and the drill with the words "create space" still ringing in my head.

Roman is working with Taylor. Checking has changed the defenceman's game immediately. The forwards are still thinking about avoiding contact with the other players, moving around them, but defencemen are doing exactly the opposite.

Ben has the puck. He skates in towards Taylor, who is facing him and skating backwards, following his movements. Ben stickhandles right, then quickly left, and Taylor begins to reach for the puck.

"Play the man!" Roman calls, but it's too late. Ben has switched back the other way and Taylor can't turn quickly enough. Ben is past him.

"Let's try it again," Roman says. "You just stay between him and the goal. Keep your eye on his chest. Forget about the puck."

"But if I'm not watching the puck, he'll put it between my legs," Taylor protests.

"That's fine," Roman says. "That's not going to do him any good if he's sitting on his can."

Ben comes in again. He dekes left, and right, and Taylor stays steady, skating backwards, keeping himself between Ben and the net. When Ben breaks for the outside, Taylor simply steps in front of him. The puck slides ahead, but Ben can't stay with it, and Taylor steadily pins him to the boards.

"There you go," Roman says.

"That was easy," Taylor says, wonder across his face.

"You can let him go now," Roman says.

"Sorry," Taylor says.

Ben, his helmet crooked, shakes himself back into shape, while Taylor, still radiating insight, springs back into place to see it work again.

• • •

I've been thinking about it all day—parking in the municipal lot, weaving through the aisles at the IGA and especially driving up the Don Valley Parkway to New Centre Ice for my second game with the Vultures. I'm beginning to see how it works. If I move into a space, I create one where I have been, and if I keep moving, I continue to create more and more space around me.

The bizarre thing is that, until now, such a big space as a hockey rink has always seemed so crowded, as if there really is nowhere to go. There are only twelve of us on the ice, and two stay in front of their nets. There should be all kinds of space, but I'm beginning to see that I have to make it appear. I have to create it.

Don, one of the leaders, is centre on my line tonight. I'm right wing again, and Chris is on the left.

We're in this game. The other leader, Noel, scored midway through the first period. We're down 2–1, but it could still go either way.

Don takes a pass along the boards. A winger from the other team is on him, but Don looks my way. Something in his look tells me to charge ahead, and he feeds me the puck as I cross the blue line, staying as close to the boards as I can.

It works. The defenceman on my side has been watching Don, and he doesn't adjust in time. I skate around him, and suddenly I'm all alone on a vast stretch of open ice. I step to the goal and shoot the puck.

It barely leaves the ice and plops like a cream puff before the goalie, who pushes it aside. My shot sucks, I see, and I make a note to work on it. I turn for the corner to get the puck again, but I never get there. The other defenceman has been just behind me all along, and now that I turn, I'm turning into him.

I'm on my back. Am I dead? Hurt? No, but I'm shocked. This is a non-contact league. It's an outrage.

"Relax," the referee says, seeing my expression. "It's incidental contact. You skated into him."

Translation: I was trying to create space, but he played the man. As it turns out, I've ended up creating space for him. He's already halfway down the ice.

It's the ying and yang of hockey. Offence is about creating space, defence about filling it. Stickhandling, deking and speed create space, checking fills it.

It's easy, I tell myself as I get up and wobble to the bench. So why is it so hard?

* * *

The select team won a beautiful game this week. I could immediately see the practices paying off. There was a give-and-go in the corner that was textbook-perfect.

The prettiest goal of the night came from Evan,* one of the new arrivals. Wesley went to the corner, where the

*Evan is a strong skater, but we have to place him carefully. In the first game he played with the team, we made the mistake of putting him on a forward line with Devin and Devlin. Arena acoustics are far from perfect. When it was time for a line change, Dave called "Devin!" and all three came off at once. The other team scored.

space was, and passed back behind him to Evan, who was waiting in front of the net with all the time in the world. Evan drilled a top corner shot that drew a collective gasp from the entire rink.

There are moments in these games when the players still look like kids. They're stacked up in gear, they're tall on their skates and they move with such confidence on the ice, but sometimes a momentary look of confusion and fear betrays them and reminds us all that they're still in the sixth grade. They like grilled cheese sandwiches and Kraft Dinner for lunch. Some of them still need help picking out what to wear in the morning.

More and more, though, there are moments when the kid seems to disappear and the man that will be steps out in full force. Evan's shot was one of those times. He and Wesley skated back to the bench wearing a mixture of pride and embarrassment, as if their bodies had just done something without asking permission.

Another was Taylor's hit.

A forward on the other team drove across the blue line and curled around towards the net. He was looking at the puck and getting ready to shoot when Taylor stepped in front of him. That's all it took.

His trainer had to come out and help him off.

Sometime over the summer, the Canadian Hockey Association changed its mind about nine-year-olds and checking.

It turned out the results of its study weren't quite as clear-cut as it seemed. After the CHA's May 2002 announcement that statistics had shown no increase in the number of injuries to kids who started checking at age nine, the CBC television program *Disclosure* looked into the findings.

"It just didn't seem to make sense," the reporter on the story, Mark Kelley, told me. *Disclosure* crunched the numbers again and came up with a completely different result. They went back to the author of the study and asked him to check his results again. He found he'd made a mistake—that, in fact, among the nine- and ten-year-olds who had been checking, there were almost four times as many injuries as in the non-checking group.

Not long after that, the CHA raised the checking age back up to eleven.

"But they're continuing this so-called 'pilot project,'" Kelley said. "And it includes competitive-level teams in four different hockey associations across the country: Saskatchewan, Newfoundland, the Ottawa District Association and the biggest one of all, the Greater Toronto Hockey League."

I called Phil McKee, the executive director of the Ontario Hockey Federation, the group overseeing the pilot project in Ottawa and the GTHL.

"We're trying to understand at what age checking can or should be introduced—at what age it is most appropriate for kids to start checking in hockey," he told me. "It's a complicated issue."

Politics and number crunching aside, for the players and families at Wesley's game this week, who watched that forward crumple to the ice while Taylor stood above him, who cheered at the hit, or yelled about it, or stood in silence with their hands drawn to their mouths waiting to see if the player would get up, and for Nathan, who wasn't at the game because we didn't need any alternates, calling it "a complicated issue" is an understatement.

Kids' hockey in Canada is a very serious business. It involves a great deal of money. Families have to be prepared to spend thousands of dollars per year in fees and equipment, drive great distances several times per week, and to miss all kinds of important events in their other, non–hockey-playing children's lives.

Once a kid is eleven years old, he takes on the huge responsibility that comes with checking. If kids are not comfortable with that, they can play in a house league.

But if kids *do* end up on a competitive-level hockey team, they have to sign a contract saying they will play exclusively for that team for the rest of the season, sometimes for multiple seasons. If kids decide they want to change that arrangement because, for example, they have a dispute with the coach, or they disagree with the team philosophy, or simply because that team isn't giving them any ice time, they have to seek a "release" from that contract. The team can refuse to grant that release; the case could then go to arbitration, but until it is settled—which can sometimes take close to an entire season—these kids are not allowed to play for that team or any other.

I don't have to worry about any of that. Playing hockey costs me relatively little. I could have joined a league that has checking if I wanted to, or one that is more serious. There are adult instructional leagues where teaching sessions precede each game. I can play with men my age, with men and women, with whomever I want. And if, for any reason, I don't like my playing situation I can go somewhere else and I might even get my money back.

The only commitment I have to hockey is that I'll play if it's fun.

• • •

The Vultures are grinning, and watching the clock. It's our fifth game of the season and we're cruising into the final minute with a 5–2 lead.

I am bursting. We are a D-league team in a crappy arena in the industrial barrens of northeastern Toronto on a Sunday night, and there is no one watching this game, but I am playing hockey, I am on a team, and we are going home with a win—our first.

I got an assist tonight. It's my first of those, too. Three simple things happened: Don passed me the puck and I kept it on my stick; I took it wide, just like Dave tells the select team; and I got around the defence. I looked over my shoulder, and there was Cliff, so I pumped a backhand pass and he drilled it home for the goal: pass, skate, pass, goal. It worked.

I did it. We did it. We won.

"Hey," Noel says as we're packing up our stuff, "that place off the lobby finally opened up today—want to give it a try?"

It's called Aladdin's Palace, but it looks as if Aladdin might still be working on it, and even then it's more like Aladdin's Garage. There is a bar, with a big wall mirror and shelves of booze, but everything else is barely up and running. The walls are bare plaster. There are construction noises buzzing from the kitchen. There are folding card tables and hard, stackable chairs in the middle of the floor.

We cluster around a table, our hockey bags stacked by the door. Brock, Daryl, Don, Noel and I are all at one end; Johnny, Mike and Joe are at the other. In between are a plate of neon-tinted Middle Eastern pickles, several bottles of beer and, because it is Aladdin's opening night, a complimentary hookah filled with sweetened, spiced tobacco.

"Like a bottle toke of Dubble Bubble," Jonathan says. All hockey teams should have it so good.

BROCK: Great assist tonight. You should have heard us yelling at you. "Shoot, Tom, shoot! Why didn't you shoot?" And then you passed and Cliff scored and I was like, "Uh . . . yeah, you could do that, too."

JOE: Brock woulda shot.

NOEL: And missed.

BROCK: Hey—who's leading in penalty minutes?

DARYL: You fell on that guy.

BROCK: He'll be more careful next time.

ME:     So, you guys didn't just meet on this team,
        right? You knew each other before?

DARYL:  Don works with Brock. Johnny married
        a girl we knew in high school, and so
        did Mike.

MIKE:   A different girl.

BROCK:  Right. Joe played with us last year. Noel
        works with Don and me, and Daryl and I
        have known each other since kindergarten.

DARYL:  He started me playing hockey.

BROCK:  Not that you ever thanked me.

DARYL:  I hated it. You know, we weren't exactly
        NHL material.

BROCK:  Not back then, anyway.

DARYL:  I quit, and we didn't play together again
        until about twenty years later, at Centennial.

BROCK:  Oh, God, remember that?

DARYL:  We were inseparable growing up, and we
        went to Centennial College at the same
        time in Scarborough. There was an
        intramural league, where each school had
        a team. I was in Advertising and we were
        short players, so I got Brock.

BROCK:  It's the kind of school that is best known
        for its Automotive and Light Industrial
        programs.

DARYL:  The Advertising student body was a little
        bit more delicate than some.

ME:     What were you called?

DARYL:   The Muffhawks.

ME:       The *what?*

DARYL:   Muffhawks.

BROCK:   We were sponsored by a strip club.

DARYL:   They were passing around a bottle of Jack
          Daniel's in the dressing room before the
          first game, so we had a couple of slugs.

BROCK:   And a cigarette.

DARYL:   It's amazing what can seem like a good
          idea at the time.

BROCK:   The game wasn't ten minutes gone before
          I was throwing up behind the bench.

DARYL:   And I laughed at him.

BROCK:   Then he threw up, too.

DARYL:   Man, those other teams were good.

BROCK:   And fast.

DARYL:   Did we win anything that year?

BROCK:   Nope. Oh, wait . . .

DARYL:   Right, right . . . That one by default . . .

The two of them look into space for a while, and Don
leans in for a beer.

"That was great tonight," he says. "When Noel hit me
with that pass at centre, I knew it was coming. I knew *he*
knew . . . that communication, knowing your teammates
enough to sense what they're thinking . . . and then when
the shot goes in and it's a job well done . . . It's an incredible feeling of satisfaction.

"This is the first organized hockey I've played since I

was a kid. I played pickup all the time, but this is different. In pickup, guys come and go, and you don't really get to know each other—you don't get that feeling of camaraderie. But here, we're all working for the same thing, and we're working at it week after week . . .

"You know, if you really look at it, there are just a few decisions, a few moves, and if you get them right and you're together, you start winning."

I can see that Don spends as much time thinking about playing as I do, and with the same intensity. I hadn't thought of myself as being any more competitive than anyone else, but Don and I do seem to be a little less laid back about it.

We're also older. The others are all in their early thirties, and most are without children.

"I'm forty-four," Don says. "I stopped playing for a few years when we had kids, so I'm finding it means more to me now. My son, Jack, is playing now, too. I keep telling him that it would be great if he got into the NHL, but his top job is be a better player than Daddy. To have better skills, have more fun, get more out of it.

"I have to wake him up at 5:30 on Saturdays, and I'll tell you right now, for me it is absolutely nothing to complain about. As soon as he hears the word 'hockey' he's out of bed like a shot. It's fantastic."

"That's the best time there is in hockey," Noel says. "When you're with your buddies, playing hockey in the hallway of some hotel on a tournament . . . That's the most fun there is."

Noel is by far the best player on the team. He's a fast skater, has great reflexes and a great shot. It's occurred to me more than once that he could be playing at a much higher level.

"How'd those skates work out tonight?" Daryl asks him.

"I really wish they fit me," he says, "but they're just too small. I can't believe my brother could ever wear them, but he used them all last year and now he's got an even smaller pair."

I ask why his brother would be going through undersized skates at a rate of one per year.

"He says it gives him better control, to have them that small," Noel says, and the table goes slightly quiet.

"He's in the NHL. He plays for the Red Wings."

I ask his name.

"Steve Thomas," Noel says, and a series of highlight-reel images flash through my mind.

Steve Thomas has played in the NHL since 1985. He is a gutsy, driving player who never, ever seemed to give up and who gave the Toronto Maple Leafs a series of playoff wins in the late '90s with overtime goals that, time and time again, he conjured out of nothing.

I still have a "hockey card" from the end of the 2000 season with Wesley's grinning, eight-year-old face on it. It came along with the regular package of photos for house-league kids. On the back of the card it lists Wesley's name, which way he shoots, what position he plays, and his favourite player. In that space, it says "Steve Thomas."

"How old is he now?" I ask.

"He's forty," Noel says.

"Is he talking about retiring?" Brock asks.

"There are guys older than that," Mike says. "I mean, [Chris] Chelios will be forty-two next year, and Mark Messier's turning forty-three."

"Hey," I say. "*I'm* turning forty-three."

"Yeah," Mike says, "but he's in the NHL. And you're in Aladdin's Palace."

There are laughs all around. The empties are cleared away. The hookah is all smoked out, and people are pushing back chairs to go.

It's still only 9 p.m.

I call Wesley to tell him about the win and my assist.

"That's great, Dad," he says, but he's tired and isn't really listening. I'm about to tell him about playing with Steve Thomas's little brother, but, in the end, I decide not to. I tell him I'll see him tomorrow.

IX

THE SELECT TEAM HAS BEEN holding skating practices at a neighbourhood rink on Tuesday mornings before school. My early-morning job keeps me from going on a regular basis, but today I'm off work. It's a cold November dawn and snow is falling.

Wesley is with his mother on Tuesday mornings. I'm here before she has dropped him off. The rink is open, but there's only a safety lamp glowing at one end, casting a grey half-light across the ice.

I take a few pucks and go out on my own.

The room is silent except for my skates. I turn a few laps, the cool air sailing through my jersey and around my legs and neck.

Dave arrives next, with Reed, his son. They are talking hockey as they step onto the ice. Their conversation turns, without stopping, into a demonstration. Dave approaches while Reed skates backwards, keeping him in position with a raised gloved hand.

"That's it," Dave says. "Just on a forty-five-degree angle. Now, come sideways in, stay between me and the net . . ."

They skate the length of the ice, face to face, talking as they go, a father and son in the early-morning light.

This scene, I realize, is a piece of Canadian mythology. It's one of those images, like a train crossing the Prairies, a horse-drawn sleigh in old Quebec, or a fishing boat steaming past Peggy's Cove, that Canadians hang on to so we can remind ourselves of how we got to be who we are.

It's easy, at times, to think those images are really just myth, that they don't really exist anywhere except in coffee-table books and election campaign commercials.

But this picture has not been posed, and it's a beautiful thing to see.

Wesley arrives, and we skate a lap together—no pucks, no passing, just the rhythmic chopping of skate blades on the ice and the steam of our breath as we go.

We've only gone around the net twice when the others start to arrive and the moment is gone, but I've already got what I came for. I smile at Wesley, he smiles back and the practice starts.

* * *

My friend Scott Sellers told me about a group that plays shinny at a rink in Mississauga on Saturday nights. Men and women of all ages play. Twenty people skate every week. There are twelve on the ice and four on each bench. You play until you're tired, and there is another player waiting to go on. It costs ten bucks.

Heather Gill organizes it. She and her husband Kevin both play, as does their son Jeff.

"Jeff used to drive the Zamboni here. That's how we got this ice time," Kevin tells me as I find a spot in the dressing room and begin to pull out my gear. He's a middle-aged man of medium size, who, just by the way he stands on his skates, looks as if he's been playing hockey since he could walk.

"We're the last ones here on Saturdays," he tells me. "We can stay on as long as we want. Sometimes that's an hour and a half, sometimes longer."

The rink is attached to a banquet hall, and this night there's a wedding reception in progress. "Sweet Home Alabama" is blaring through the walls and leaking into the dressing room.

There are ten or twelve men in the room with us, one or two in their thirties, most in their mid-forties and a couple of others older than that. Beside me on the bench are two teenaged boys, tying their skates.

We chat as I find my shin pads and pull on my socks. The one next to me is Colin. He's fourteen.

"I play Bantam 'A' in Meadowvale," he tells me. "It's two practices and two games a week. It's pretty good." And he leans into a bent knee, stretching the other leg out behind.

"Where did you hear about this game?" I ask.

"Our friends Doug and Shannon called us," the other one says. "His mom couldn't make it."

"We're filling in for her," Colin says.

Kevin is on his way out to warm up. He makes a final count to confirm that he's balanced the teams.

"John," he says to a late-forties man by the door, "you're in a white jersey, okay?

John nods.

"Uh . . ." And he looks at me, forgetting my name.

"Tom."

"Right. You got a dark jersey?"

I have. Kevin looks around one more time and sees the teenagers.

"Oh, yeah, no hitting. Right, you guys? Heather talked to you?"

"Yeah. She met us out in the lobby," one says.

"Sure," Colin echoes. "That's cool. No hitting."

"Keep your head up, anyway," one of the older guys warns, and there is a second of silence before the two boys stop and look around warily. Everybody laughs.

We have a few minutes to warm up. I can see that one or two of the players are clearly beginners and just learning to skate. A few others have that solid, level stride of strength and experience.

I turn a few laps and take a seat on the bench as the game gets underway. My friend Scott is at the other end of the bench, Colin, the teenager, is next along, and right beside me is Heather Gill.

"I started this game as a way of getting us all together

on the weekends," she says. "The family's so busy that this is one way we can be sure we're together and having fun. That's one of the big reasons I started playing in the first place. Everyone else did. There was my husband, Kevin, my son, Jeff, and our daughter, Jennifer. I was spending all that time at the arena and I finally decided to use some of it for myself."

Heather is not a big woman. She's no more than five foot two and her head looks slightly lost inside her helmet and face cage.

"Jennifer's going to be nineteen this fall. That was another reason. I mean, it used to be a girl/boy thing. Once she was playing, I'd see her looking at me and wondering why I was the only one who wasn't. I didn't want the reason to be 'Because I'm a woman.'"

There's a banging on the boards at the other end of the bench, and it's my turn to play.

The puck is in the other team's end and I can see a space on defence, so that's where I go. A woman on the other team digs it out of the corner and turns up along the boards, passing to a forward who is curling through centre ice and into our zone.

It is Heather's son, Jeff. He's tall and slim, with arms that look about six inches too long. I'm jockeying him, skating backwards, but he's got great acceleration, and with that impossible reach he's almost got the puck around me while he's still on the other side. I'm turned around all over my skates and have become a pylon for Jeff to fly around, when out of nowhere another player shoots in behind me, cuts Jeff off and steals the puck.

It is Kevin, Jeff's dad, who winks at his son before rifling the puck off the boards and out of the zone.

"Show-off," Jeff says as he skulks back across the line.

"Gotta keep an eye on him," Kevin says, with a look of pride that could be for either of them.

Jeff heads for the bench and another player leaps on. He's wearing a brown jersey and is strong on his skates. He pokes the puck away from our forward and is soon bearing down on me.

I'm skating backwards, trying to angle the player off to the boards, when he puts on another burst of speed and, just like Jeff, gets around me and is gone. Kevin comes across again, but this time he's too late and the new player drills a high wrist shot that gets past our goalie on the glove side.

The other team cheers, but this isn't a game anyone is trying to win and it's clear that no one is keeping score. Still, I feel a little sheepish. This is the first time I have played in full equipment and not been the worst player on the ice. I'd been enjoying that feeling of competence when I completely misjudged this new player's speed and ability.

I head to the bench. I sit down beside a middle-aged woman and let out a sigh.

"Man," I say, "that guy is good."

She looks at me, clears her throat in a knowing way, and smiles wide.

"That's no guy," she says. "That's Sue."

I laugh out loud.

"You're not the first one to get caught like that," she says.

I have no doubt.

* * *

After the game, we gather at a nearby restaurant for beer and food. Sue, who beat me so thoroughly and whom I spent the rest of the night watching like a hawk, hasn't come along because her competitive-level women's team has a game tomorrow night and she's making sure she has enough rest.

"Sue's a serious player," Kevin Gill tells me. "In the past few years we've seen the level of play in the women's leagues come way, way up. She's always been good, but now there are 'A' and 'B' leagues, so she's playing with whole teams of players that are just as good as she is, and she's getting better every week."

Kevin is sitting beside Heather. Jeff, their twenty-one-year-old son, is in the corner, across from John, digging into an enormous plate of nachos.

"You had a good game," John says to Heather. "At least that can opener you gave me was the best I've seen in a long time."

"Oh, come on," Heather says. "I was reaching for the puck."

"Perfect can opener," John goes on. "I was still admiring it after I fell."

"You guys never used to give me this kind of trouble," Heather complains.

"You never used to give me can openers . . ."

"Playing with these guys all the time has been really good for me," Heather says as the beer arrives. "The first time, somebody lifted my stick. I still remember this—I was carrying it up the boards and I was really happy that I could carry it that well, and then a stick appears from behind and jerks my blade off the ice, and then she skates away with it and I'm like, 'Hey, that's mine!' I was really thinking she'd been totally rude to me . . . but that's not what this is about. You learn that's part of the game. You learn those rules for behaviour don't apply in the game. You're allowed here—you're allowed to play hard and do what you need to. You don't have to hold it all in. It's kind of liberating, you know? It's good to know that if you get a goal or make a good play, nobody's giving it to you. You have to work and fight for it, and if you get it, it's really yours."

Another player joins us. He was on my team and we shared a few shifts together. He is a beautiful skater, quick-footed and nimble, always cycling through the open spaces. His name is Nori Takahashi.

I ask him where he learned to skate.

"I started playing when I was nineteen," he says. "I was at Chiba University, in Tokyo.

"We had no coach or professor at the university. There was no hockey program. We were just a group of students who were interested. I went to the library and got some books and videos and we taught ourselves.

"Ice time is extremely expensive in Tokyo. For just ninety minutes you have to pay over five hundred U.S. dollars. It's very tough and we had to work very hard off the ice to get the most out of our experience. When the company I worked for, Canon, brought me to Canada. I was excited. I love hockey and I was sure it would be easy for me to play here.

"It wasn't easy. I used email before I left to try and find a team, but there was nothing. Then, when I got here, I found a place to live very close to a big arena in Mississauga. I tried to find a team there at my level, but it was the middle of the season and there were no spaces. I was looking at the winter going by with no hockey at all.

"Then I heard about shinny games that people organize on their own, like this one, and I started going to rinks to see what I could find. I always brought my equipment with me so I would be ready, but it was still hard.

"I told people I came from Japan, that I had played for ten years, but they thought I would be a bad player. I was very upset. We had a very good team in Japan. We worked very hard. We were good.

"I heard about this game and came to see Kevin, and he said I could play maybe the next week. He asked if I needed skates. It was funny to me. I mean, they really thought I would be a beginner. I arrived very early and was all ready to go, and as soon as we had started playing, Kevin turned to me and he said, 'Hey, you're really good!'

"I scored a goal that night. Now I'm here every week.

"I couldn't speak English very well, but I could play hockey. I just needed a chance to prove it."

Janice, the goalie on the other team, has joined us.

"I only started playing after I turned forty, and I was just like you," she says, looking at Heather. "I started because I'd been hauling kids around all the time, playing hockey, and I thought, 'Why not me?' Then, my second son's team had a mother/son game at the end of the year. They needed a goalie and I had equipment that sort of fit, so I did it, and I had such a blast. I've really never stopped playing since.

"The kids' father plays hockey as well. He always did. That's how the boys got started, but that was a long time ago. We've been divorced thirteen years.

"Girls didn't do sports when I was growing up, and I didn't have any brothers, so that was that, but I always wanted to do it. I always wanted to play. This is really a latent desire I'm acting on."

I ask her how much the divorce had to do with bringing out that latent desire.

"Actually, there was one time when I really felt it and knew I had to act. It was just after we split up; I was driving home from a game, with all four kids in the car—and the littlest was still small enough to be in a stroller. We stopped at a convenience store because they were thirsty after their game, and it was going to be a while before we got home, so I sent the oldest two into the store to get drinks.

"Well, they came out with four drinks, one for each of the kids, and I'd given them enough money for five. 'What about me?' I asked. 'Oh, we didn't think of you,' they said, and that's when it kind of hit me. I was a nonentity. It was a real wake-up call, and I was thinking, 'You know what? I matter, too.'

"After that, anytime I did something for them, I did something for myself. I guess one of those things was to start playing hockey.

"It means so much to me now. It's physical and mental and social. I'm in as good shape now as I ever was, and the best thing is that they think it's cool that I play. I remember taking my younger son to get new skates, and he was behind me, talking with the clerk. 'Hey,' I heard him say. 'My mum plays hockey.' He was bragging. That made me feel really good."

• • •

The select team got some bad news this week. Devlin chipped his kneecap playing basketball in the schoolyard. He might be back by late February.

There isn't anything good about this news, but it does bring about something of a positive situation for the three players on the alternate list. They'll be seeing a lot more action, and tonight, in Downsview Arena, Wesley is playing with Nathan once again.

The Downsview team has not been as strong this year. Joseph, last year's standout centre, is not on the squad, and Leaside has won both games the teams have played this season. However, where the first was an easy win, and the second was less so, this game, going into the third period, is very, very close. We are losing 2–1.

The introduction of checking is working out well for Downsview. They have several stocky players who are making sure nothing comes easily to Leaside.

It has taken until now, two months into the season, for bodychecking to begin to really have an effect. Nathan, however, hasn't had as many chances to play, and if that inexperience happens to show itself as he skates past one of those natural checkers with his head down, he could end up really hurt.

That hasn't happened. He and Wesley are happy to be playing together again, and midway through the third period, it is Nathan, sneaking in beside a very big Downsview defenceman, who takes a pass from Wesley across the crease and scores to tie the game.

Wesley is grinning towards the bench as they come back to centre for the face-off. He is looking at me, at Dave, at Nathan's father in the crowd. As far as he is concerned, without any ill will to Devlin, this is exactly the way things are supposed to be.

Still, the game gets more intense. Within three minutes of Nathan's goal, the Downsview team throws no fewer than ten enormous checks, each one drawing a primal yawp from the home crowd.

Derek is sent skidding, Taylor thumped to the ice, Andrew crushes a forward into the boards and only seconds later switches roles from crusher to crushee. Excitement seeps into the players' voices, and when it is their turn to go on, they burst from the gate, gripping their sticks like pitchforks.

With two minutes to go, Wesley's line goes on for a face-off in the Downsview zone, and thirty seconds later they have possession and are closing in. Evan, the right winger, moves for the net and is checked by a defenceman, but as he stumbles he makes a clever drop pass to Nathan, ten feet out at the right side of the net.

Nathan can shoot. He has a chance, but in those tiny instants as he looks, with that same beefy defenceman now charging his way, Nathan sees Wesley across the crease, facing an open net. Nathan waits a moment longer, and as the roar from the Downsview crowd reverberates off the rafters of the arena, just before that defenceman drives into his chest and sends him flying backwards, Nathan lets the pass go.

The puck lands on Wesley's stick and Nathan, still watching when Wesley's hands go up in celebration, lets out a whoop as he flops to the ice.

• • •

I am pumped for the Vultures' game this week. I have seen what passing can do. I have seen what courage can do. I have seen how victory can feel and I want it. I want to see the puck slip past the goaltender and gently tug against the back of the net before it falls in slow motion to the ice. I want to win.

I strikes me that I've always wanted that. It is a fundamental Canadian fantasy.

I blared Led Zeppelin in the basement, felt the drive of that searing, rhythmic mayhem, and saw myself on stage as if that really were me up there burning out guitar solos instead of Jimmy Page.

I could feel the softness of Leslie's lips against mine as clearly as if she were pressed right next to me, the gentle curve of her back beneath my hands and her golden hair cascading over my arms.

And I could feel the weight of the Stanley Cup in my hands as I skated the victory lap around the Montreal Forum, hoisting the Cup high, with Bob Gainey, Larry Robinson and Yvan Cournoyer cheering me, all of us following the greatest gentleman the game has ever seen, Jean Beliveau.

I never learned to play the guitar. I never even tried.

Leslie dated Peter all the way through high school and was never remotely interested in me. At least, I don't think she was. I never asked.

Beliveau never played alongside Gainey and Robinson—he'd retired by the time they joined the Habs—and even then it would have looked pretty funny to see me out there at only twelve years old, especially since I'd quit hockey four years before and couldn't turn to the right.

No matter. Playing rock 'n' roll, kissing the prettiest girl, scoring the goal and winning the Stanley Cup. We talk ourselves out of these dreams because we know they're impossible, but the dreams never truly die, and as life slips through our fingers those old dreams start to scream all the louder for their place in our lives.

I've lived the reasonable dreams. Some of them came true, and a whole lot didn't, and now, goddammit, I want the one I wanted all along. I want to play hockey. I want to be on the team. I want to score goals. I want to win the championship.

The outdoor rinks are open again, and I'm very happy to say that I've improved in the past year. I can make a few passes now, and I can skate backwards well enough to box forwards out of the play. I see the patterns more often, and once in a while I can feel myself making those decisions that happen so quickly they don't ask my permission first.

I played twice this week. Yesterday morning, Dave held a fast, hard-driving select practice. I performed every drill, and now, as I'm lacing up my skates in the dressing room at New Centre Ice before this week's Vultures game, my legs feel as if they might jump off my body and skate away on their own.

The confidence takes a while to settle in. I'm reacting, and skating, and seeing the play, but still, it's the end of the first period before I begin to jump on the ice without the usual clamour of instructions in my head.

In the second period, things are clearer still. I'm finding speed I didn't know was there. I'm getting to the puck before I expect to, and finding time to feel what to do with it when I do.

And then, in the third period, it finally happens. Daryl is in the corner. I move to the far side of the net at the same time as he charges. The defence follows him. He passes to me.

I feel it and see it over and over again in my mind. It's as if I'm watching myself. My stick cradles the puck. I wind up a little, even though the open net is only inches away. I see the puck cross the goal line and watch it there on the other side of the mesh. Heat spreads from my feet up through my legs to my shoulders and right up to my face as I throw back my head and I roar.

The only part that is different from the dream is how it feels afterwards. In the dream, after the goal and the win, I'm truly satisfied. But as I drive south along the Don Valley Parkway, the lights floating past and the buzz still rising through my face, it's clear that what happened tonight is just the beginning. I want more.

* * *

I am on the subway on a Saturday morning, going to Ramsden Park to play shinny.

My skates and helmet are in the bag at my feet and my stick is planted on the floor. The man sitting across from me leans forward. He is in his early forties, and wearing a very bulky down-filled jacket done all the way up to the collar. Struggling slightly with what is obviously a second language, he asks if I am going to play, and he hesitates before he says it, "hockey?"

I say yes, I am. He asks how the game works, if it is hard, and where he might learn how to play. He moved to Toronto in August, he says, in middle of a heat wave, from Guatemala. He was told about the cold, and, he confides, had been warned that the people might seem unfriendly at first, and that it might take him a year until he knew enough of his neighbours to begin to feel at home. Nobody said anything, though, about the game that consumes so much of the country's time, money and thought.

"It is important thing here," he says. And then, looking me over, he asks if I am a teacher.

I laugh, but it occurs to me that I could teach him something.

I tell him what I can: that it is a fast game, that skating is important, that it is very difficult to play well, but that most players are tolerant with beginners. I tell him that I am still a beginner myself.

I ask if he has ever skated.

"I would like to," he says, smiling at me as I get up to go. He looks encouraged. I wish him luck and urge him to give it a try.

It's my first time at this rink. Ramsden Park is nestled at the northwestern edge of Rosedale, one of Toronto's wealthiest neighbourhoods. My friend Greig Clarke told me about this game. He comes here every Saturday in the winter with a group of friends, most of whom have played hockey together since their university days.

One is Paddy, who might be in his mid-fifties. He has

a tight grin and a rosy face topped by a mop of hair that is almost white. He played for the University of Massachusetts and was a two-time All-American in the seventies. Another is Cam, who is nearing sixty and is tall with silver hair. Cam played professionally in Europe, in an era when, on nights off, he and the other first-line players on his team would hire themselves out on a game-by-game basis to hockey clubs in neighbouring cities, often to face the same team they'd just finished beating on their home ice the night before.

The game is already in progress when I arrive, and for a moment I wonder if I've come on the wrong day. I don't recognize any of the players as people I've met before, and none of them look old enough to be Cam or Paddy.

I make my way to the bench, searching faces and watching the play. It's a beautiful game. The skating is quick. The passes are smart, and the players seem to all be finding room to move, so that even when they are sprinting for the puck, the motion is smooth and graceful. When somebody makes a good play, both benches cheer.

There is a helmet rule on public rinks that is strictly enforced at all the shinny games I've played, but it is clearly not in effect here. Many of these players learned the game when nobody wore a helmet. They have toques or caps, and one has a red beret, pushed rakishly to one side.

It's a scene out of a nostalgic painting: old-time hockey played by lifelong friends.

A player floats by the bench in a red, white and blue Canadiens-style jersey, and as I really look at his face I see it is Cam. And, on another look, I see Paddy across the ice, sprinting up the boards.

Their features are the same as they were the last time I saw them, away from the ice, but here they both look ten years younger. Neither is wearing a hat. The wind is blowing through their hair and they look as carefree, I'm sure, as the day they met, decades earlier, as young men.

This ice is the same as in any rink, anywhere else in the city, but there is something very different about this *game*. Players are skating full out, and they're making some terrific plays, but whatever urgency there is, is only in the game. It's hockey, and nothing else.

Shinny games in other places have often seemed to me to have an intensity or an anger that could easily have more to do with all of the other struggles the players bring with them when they put on their skates. They act out their conflicts on the ice, and leave their anger there.

There is none of that here, and I can only think of two reasons how that could be. One is that, for these players, hockey is a way to escape all of that for a while, and return to a simpler time in their lives. It also could be just the same, here, as anywhere else, except that these players just don't have to struggle as much off the ice.

They've already won those games.

• • •

I go to Regent Park, to the outdoor rink on the south side of Dundas, on a Friday evening just after six. I'm expecting to see the chalet full of kids pulling on equipment, the "organized chaos" Dexter Slater described to me last year.

There are three kids in full gear on the ice, along with two teenaged girls standing by the boards, one beside a boyfriend, and a guy in a parka without skates, standing in snow boots alone at centre ice, drilling wrist shots at the boards. There is also a stocky kid wearing jeans and a jacket, with no helmet or gloves, skating with a stick and puck up and down the ice. He's got a tough look about him and a crooked smile as he buzzes past the teenagers and pokes at the boyfriend a few times.

After a minute, he swoops towards the goal and takes a slap shot. It's a hard, rising shot that clanks off the centre post in the back of the net. He's a powerful player. The kid corrals the puck and buzzes by the teenagers again.

This is supposed to be the Friday-night hockey program that gathered together the busload of kids and families that were so enthusiastic at the outdoor tournament Wesley took part in two years ago.

The chalet is almost empty.

I find the person in charge, a woman named Carlotta, and ask where all the kids are.

"We're in a rebuilding phase right now," she says with an apologetic smile. "The kids just aren't coming out in the same numbers this year. You really can't tell from Friday to Friday how it's going to turn out. We've got all kinds of equipment here in the back room. All the kids have to do is show up and ask, but it was really warm today, so I guess a lot of them aren't coming. They'll come out when it's cold again, like it was last week. We had two full teams then, but when it's nice, they seem to find other things they want to do."

I ask what there is for the kids who do show up—is there any program for them?

"No, there really isn't. They practise and play around, and they can still come out, even if they're the only one, but that's all we can do for them if there isn't enough for a game."

"Aren't there other kids who'd like to play?" I ask.

"Oh, yes. We had forty kids out every week last year, but a lot of them were twelve years old and so they're too old for the program now. There's nothing for them once they turn thirteen."

"Nothing at all?" I ask.

"They used to have a program for thirteen- and fourteen-year-olds, but they had trouble with kids fighting, so they phased it out. It was really getting out of hand. Parents would come to watch, and see their kids fighting each other. It wasn't good, so the city eliminated it."

By this time, only two of the kids in equipment are on the ice. The teenagers have gone, leaving the stocky kid, who is charging back and forth again with the puck, firing at the boards and the fence and looking around for others.

"He was in the program last year," Carlotta tells me. "He came out every week. Now he's too old. He still helps out with some of the little kids when we need it, but otherwise he can't play. It's too bad."

I look at him again and he begins to look familiar. I can't be sure, but he looks very much like the tough and gritty captain of the Regent Park team at those tournaments, the one who scored so many goals and dominated the games.

He comes off the ice and clomps into the chalet.

Another kid comes off the ice.

"What about the city-wide tournaments, like two years ago at Giovanni Caboto and Maple Leaf Gardens?" I ask. "Is the city still running those?"

Carlotta lowers her voice. "They're going to be eliminated," she says.

"Funding cutbacks?" I ask.

"Yeah," she says, shaking her head. "That's what it is."

The boyfriend is back now, all by himself. He is wearing a matching fleece jacket and toque with a hockey team logo across the front. He looks about sixteen, and I'm guessing he plays for a high-level team somewhere. He tosses a puck into the corner and charges after it— quick, strong strides—the length of the ice, finishing up with a rocket of a wrist shot into the top corner. He picks up the puck then, jams it in a pocket, skates back off the ice and walks into the chalet to take off his skates.

Dexter Slater told me that, every year, a few kids from Regent get to play for competitive-level teams when a sponsor will cover the fees.

He also told me about one player he knew of from the

neighbourhood who made it to the big leagues: Glenn Metropolit.

"I grew up with him," Dexter said. "He banged away at it all winter, every winter, out there on the rink after school. He played in the East Coast League, then in Portland for the AHL, and he made it to the bigs—you know, a kid from Regent. He came from the same kind of economic background that I came from. He was the one who made it."

Glenn Metropolit played for the Washington Capitals for a few years, then in the minors a couple more, and then ended up in Europe, where he is today.

Metropolit came from a difficult situation. His father abandoned his mother before Glenn was born. His adoptive father served jail time when Glenn was a child, and Glenn's brother is currently serving a lengthy sentence for his part in a brutal kidnapping and home invasion in 1999. The victims were a wealthy Rosedale couple.

The sportswriters who write about Metropolit praise his dedication to succeed despite the circumstances of his childhood. It's another Canadian myth: the hard-scrabble kid who claws his way to the top with raw determination and a heart of gold.

But for most kids from this neighbourhood, banging away is the only thing they can do, and living the myth is far from a sure thing.

I'm turning to go when I hear a rhythmic *whack-whack-whack* from inside the chalet. It's the stocky kid, the one who showed such promise two years ago, and who captained his team to two successive city-wide championship games held in an NHL arena, but who is no longer allowed to play because he's older than twelve. He is sitting on a bench between two others about his age, who stare ahead at the floor, bored, while he slaps his hockey stick on the floor, again and again, raising it higher every time, the clap of the impact echoing through the empty chalet.

Carlotta walks over to talk to him, and the three get up to leave. They go without speaking, hands stuffed in pockets, and they push through the door and away from the rink into the night. Not one of them looks back.

X

I'VE TAKEN THE NEXT STEP, and the next. I'm taking
step after step, my left foot crossing over my right, as
I go very slowly around the face-off circle at New
Centre Ice.

It's more than two weeks since my goal with the
Vultures. I've played shinny five times, had two more
Vultures games and even helped out in a scrimmage at
the select practice this week, but haven't come close to
that moment since. My shots have been weak, my passes
lame. It's as if all my meagre hockey skills piled on top of
themselves for that one instant of glory, and now there's
nothing left.

I've called David Trombley, the skating coach we've
hired to run the Tuesday-morning practices for the
select team. He runs his own hockey training school
called Hockey Extreme.

He is a rare teacher. He can break down the elements of skating into small, understandable tasks and explain them in a way that is always positive. Because of that, he can charge a lot of money for an hour of his time, and people like me will pay it.

It's not as if he's overcharging. In fact, given his training and ability and the demands on his time, I'm pretty sure he's giving me a deal, but it still feels indulgent. After worrying all last winter about whether I was ready to start using my "expensive" stick, the one that cost more than ten dollars, I've now spent almost twelve times that for a single hour of instruction.

I am not thinking about that right now, though. In fact, the whole issue of cost has vanished from my mind. I am focused on my toes, on pointing them as I step, left foot over right. I am keeping my hips square and my bum down, trying to balance evenly on each blade as my weight transfers slowly from one to the other.

That's what Dave has me doing: crossing my left over my right and leaving both blades on the ice for a second or two, gliding with my legs crossed to exaggerate and take apart the weight transfer. It's working. I can feel each of the muscles taking the weight in turn—some, it seems, for the very first time.

When I arrived, Dave told me to skate a lap, and I hadn't finished my first turn, a wrong-side crossover, before he pointed something out. He noticed that, as I cross my left foot over my right, I'm flat-footed. My left was landing on the ice with a clunk and the left blade was not in line with my right. It was costing me speed and balance the instant it touched the ice.

So Dave told me to point my toes. I felt the difference instantly, and, in that same instant, decided that whatever this was costing me was worth it.

My teacher, however, has more to teach. Next, we are on to stopping.

I press all of my weight on the foot that leads into the stop, while the other foot, especially on my wrong-side stop, is dangling behind uselessly. Dave tells me I am neglecting to use my inside edge. I didn't know I *had* an inside edge, and, as it turns out, I don't.

We work on that, and soon I am gliding on one blade, lightly sliding the flat of the other along the ice at a right angle, as if it is frosting a cake, gradually sliding it forward and leaning on it with more and more weight. I finish in what looks like a ballet pose: my right foot turned out, supporting all my weight, my left foot in a point behind it.

Again, the drill finds new muscles, and soon I have a very feeble, but still detectable, inside-edge stop.

We work on shooting. The tendency for the beginning shooter, Dave says, is to clamp down to get a harder shot—to enlist every muscle in the entire upper body from the fingers to the shoulders in the effort.

"You end up like a player in a table-hockey game," he says, swivelling stiffly around in one awkward swoop to demonstrate. "You've got the butt of your stick jammed into your ribs—it can hardly move. But look at all of these thousands of muscles in your hands, in your wrists. Look how fluid they can be. You're treating your arm like a pile driver when it could be a slingshot. Let each of those muscles do their part, one after the other. Make it even." He corrals a puck and, as smoothly as if he's casting a fly rod, sends the puck in a single, graceful motion all the way from windup to release.

The shot clangs off the crossbar with such force that it bounces straight up and gets caught in the rafters hanging over the rink.

The hour is over in no time, but nobody is using the ice right away, so I am left on my own to digest what I've learned.

My head is swimming.

I haven't tried to master a new physical challenge like this in about twenty-five years, when I was first studying to be a musician. This is very much the same. Like music, hockey is played in time—things have to happen at a precise instant or it's too late. It is intuitive, it's communicative, and it involves mastering an almost infinite number of specific, detailed skills and putting them together with others in the moment.

I am remembering that obsessive thirst for knowledge and the joy of discovering a new ability, just as it was when I was practising my trombone at tenth-grade band camp. I am literally entranced by this new, inside-edge stopping drill. It gives me such confidence to feel a small amount of control where I had none before, and it is terrific to want something this much again. I do it over and over and over.

I do it the next afternoon at the outdoor rink.

I do it during the breaks at the Leaside practice that Saturday morning.

I do it while the others are dividing up the sticks for shinny at Dieppe Park that Sunday afternoon.

But the following Wednesday, after another ninety minutes at New Centre Ice, I find myself sighing all the way home.

It's not for lack of motivation. I am just as obsessed as ever, and even hungrier for progress. I'm sharing hockey lessons with three other men now. We're learning more from Dave Trombley than any of us can absorb in a single session anyway, and it is good to work with others.

The trouble is that, just as I am learning a wealth of new skills, I can't help but see how much more there is left to learn. Whatever initial progress I felt hasn't even come close to keeping up with my ambition. My stops are marginally better, but I can now see how they should be twice as good. My crossovers are the same. My stick-handling is even weaker. I have a very, very long way to go.

In the latter part of a lesson, one of the other students, Gary, takes a pass along the boards and quickly drops it back to Dave, our teacher, behind him.

"That's a great pass!" Dave enthuses. "You took a look before and knew I'd still be there. Think slowly and act fast. That's real hockey sense."

The words land like lead in my stomach. It's the unspoken fear I've had all along: that I don't have any hockey sense—that no matter how much I improve the *elements* of my game, my intuitive understanding, my ability to feel and see the play unfold will never really be there.

I can find all the support I need for that fear in the one part of my game that matters most to me, the one that is still the farthest away: passing. To send a puck so that it lands on the stick of another speeding player requires a very subtle calculation. It's what I want to be able to do more than anything, but at the instant of release, when inspiration turns into action, my arms tighten, my vision locks. Time and time again I watch as the puck I have sent goes nowhere near where I want it to be.

The drive to make it work burns stronger in me every time I play. I love that communication, that fleeting magic that emerges from ice and nothing to draw a wire of connection from one person to another.

That's what "hockey sense" means to me, and the player I most want to connect with has it in spades. "Hockey sense" is what appeared, all of a sudden, on Lac Croche when Wesley saw the patch of ice between my legs and sent the puck that way. It's what led him to leave that wonderful drop pass for Andrew, to charge the puck away from Joseph and use it to draw the Downsview goalie from the net. To connect like that with him is what I crave more than anything in the world.

Connection used to be so much a part of our lives that we didn't even know it was there. I wouldn't even have called it "connection" when we lived in the same house. It was life.

I've come to hockey to try and rediscover that intuitive, unspoken connection, but like most of my passes, this one feels as if it's far too late.

• • •

The Vultures won tonight. Don scored twice early on, then Noel scored another two. By the third period we were winning 5–1 and things started getting ugly. There were shoving matches and slashing penalties. A defenceman knocked me over in front of their net, and when I got up I was yelling things that I wouldn't repeat anywhere else.

The celebration in the change room is subdued. Winning is more fun than losing, but winning like this isn't that much fun somehow, and everyone says as much as we pull off our gear.

At least, almost everyone does.

Bruce is a good goalie, and he's kept us in many a game when nothing else did, but off the ice he's barely part of the team. He plays for two other groups every week and probably can't name any of them, or us. He is the first to leave most nights, and he usually does in silence. His voice is high and pinched, and the most I've heard it all year has been either in complaints to the referee or the weekly stream of abuse he aims at Big Joe.

Joe is six foot eight on skates. He's got a friendly, booming voice, and he seems to have more stories and jokes at the ready than anyone else in the dressing room, most of them told while he's stark naked and halfway to the shower.

"This is an incredible bunch of guys," he told me early on. "I've played on teams that are nowhere near as much fun as this. There are puck hogs and jerks who get on you if you're not on your game . . . We're unbelievably lucky. There isn't one person on this team that you wouldn't want to hang out with, anyway.

"Well, okay," he said with a glint in his eye. "There might be *one*."

The issue between Bruce and Joe, it seems, is personal space. Bruce, understandably, likes to be able to see shots before they come his way, and he finds that difficult when Big Joe, in all his bigness, is in his line of sight. On the other hand, Joe is a defenceman. One of his jobs is to clear the other team's forwards out of the goalie's way, and it's difficult to do that without stepping into the fray.

"Asshole," Joe mutters after Bruce bundles out with his gear bagged up. "Did you see what he did to me tonight? He actually slashed me, right on the back of my calf. I've got this big galoot from the other team bearing down on me, and then I feel this hack on the leg from my own teammate! Look, there's a bruise like a grapefruit starting up. What the hell is that?"

"Now, Joe," Brock says, "I'm sure Bruce would be happy to discuss things calmly before the next game."

"Yes, Joseph," Daryl smiles. "Give him a call. Maybe you two could get together for a latte during the week."

"Or a salad," says Mike.

"Bite me," Joe retorts, the grin creeping back to his face before he turns and clumps away to the shower.

• • •

It's late on a Saturday night and I'm pulling out of the parking lot at Vic Johnston Arena in Streetsville, Ontario, on the way to a watering hole down the street. I've just spent ninety minutes mistiming passes and not quite catching opportunities with the Gill family and friends at their Saturday-night shinny game.

The low point of the night came when Scott, who has been playing about as long as I have and is a lot better, beat me to the puck three times in a row on essentially the same play. We were stuck in our own end and the puck came ripping around the boards. I saw it coming and went for it, but before I could get there, Scott picked it off and slid a beautiful pass to Jeff in front of our net. The third time, Jeff scored. I felt that ugly drive surge up in me and was hunkering down to get it right this time, no matter what, when I caught a look from Kevin Gill. He'd been watching me, and his face clearly told me that he'd been there, too, and things weren't likely to improve with me feeling the way I was.

I went to the bench.

"I started playing in Verdun, in Montreal, when I was six or seven years old," Kevin tells me as a plate of nachos arrives with a new pitcher of beer. "Verdun had a lot of outdoor rinks, and in those days it was cold enough to play for months. That's where we learned. Some nights it was so cold you had to go into the shed between shifts. Kids were crying because they're feet were frozen. You had to really, really like playing hockey.

"When we got older, they moved our house-league games into the new, indoor arenas, but we still played pickup on those same outdoor rinks right through school. We'd go after school, head home for dinner and come back again after that.

"The old guy who worked for the city taking care of the ice—you know, hosed it down and worked the lights? We called him 'Pop.' We called them all Pop. Each rink had an old guy who did that, and they were all Pop to us.

"Anyway, when Pop finished his shift, he gave us a key to the shed and showed us how to turn out the lights. I mean, we were fifteen and sixteen years old. He could have been fired, but we never let anyone mess the place up or anything like that. It was incredible for us. We'd stay there 'til midnight most nights and close up on our own. It was like we had our own private rink.

"I met Heather skating there," he says, looking her way. She is at the other end of the long table with Alicia, our goalie Al, and Sue, the great playmaker who beat me so thoroughly the last time I came out.

"I stopped playing for a while after Heather and I got married, but then we moved to Toronto and everybody I knew was on a team somewhere. That was twenty years ago, and I've been playing a couple of times a week ever since.

"There was a year or two when our son Jeff played with me in a men's league. We were in the top division and the playing was pretty intense at times. Jeff had been playing 'AAA' all through school until he was too old and had nowhere to play. He wasn't supposed to be in the men's leagues until he was eighteen, but he was good enough, so we lied about his age and signed him up.

"I was always looking out for him. You know, he's a fast skater and could make a real difference, and some of those guys get pretty hot-headed, and they were big, too, so if they gave him a hard time I'd step in. That's my kid, right? Even if he's an adult, part of me still sees him as a school kid, so if some big lummox starts pushing him around I'd be in there in a flash.

"Well, a few years later, guess what? I was a little slower than I used to be and Jeff was a little more filled out. One night I was playing defence, and some guy was clogging up the crease, so I got him the hell out of there and he didn't like it. He comes after me, and I'm just getting around to responding when Jeff comes in and takes him out. *Bam!* The guy went down like he was made of plastic.

"After that, Jeff was standing up for *me*.

"I eventually switched to an over-forty league. It's fast hockey—good passing, heads-up play, and none of that crap. You knock somebody down, you ask if he's all right. You pat him on the back, maybe help him up, and away you go. You know, if your body's older and you want to keep playing, you think about that stuff. What's more important: winning now or being able to play again next year?"

"That's why he plays with us," Sue says from across the table. "It's so much more civilized when we women are playing."

The others howl.

"How *does* it change when women and men play together?" I ask.

"It's a totally different game," Heather says. "Most guys are reluctant to really hit a female player, but when it's just women, it's brutal. I have more fun in the coed games."

"Everybody does," Alicia says.

"Except the guys," Sue puts in. "We play in coed tournaments a couple of times a year and it can get pretty rough for the guys. The girls on the other team are always going after them."

"You mean, trying to hit them?" I ask.

"Yeah," Sue says. "The girls go after the guys, and the guys go after the guys, too."

"The guys don't go after the girls?"

"Not if they want to leave in one piece," Kevin says. "Remember that time?" he asks Sue.

"Yup," Sue says.

"Oh, yeah," Al says, replaying it in his mind. "That was a bad scene."

"There was a fight?" I ask.

"He blindsided me," Sue says. "The puck wasn't even there. I was curling around, looking back at the play, and he hit me so hard I went flat on my back. My boyfriend, Todd, went after him."

"Todd's a big boy," Al says. "You know that guy regretted it."

"Kevin beat the hell out of him, too," Heather says. "It was supposed to be a good-natured, fun kind of game. The tournament was raising money for breast cancer, for crying out loud, and then the idiot does that."

"Some people get a little wrapped up in it," Al says. "I mean, Sue's a great player. She's scoring goals all the time. I guess he figured they weren't going to win if she was still playing."

"So he was really trying to injure you?" I ask Sue.

"Absolutely," Kevin says. "It was totally obvious. It was after the play had gone by. He just decked her, so Todd came in and levelled the guy. It cleared both benches. The ref sent everybody home, but as we were leaving he skated over to me and said, 'I'm glad you guys did that, because if you didn't, I was going to.'"

I ask if there are ever fights like that when it's just women.

"Oh, yes," Heather says. "There are a couple you really don't want to mess with."

"It's changed a whole lot," Alicia says. "When I first started playing, most of us thought we were supposed to behave a certain way. It was just part of who we were as women. If you got knocked down, the other player would say, 'Oh, are you okay?' and help you up. But then the players started getting better, or maybe the athletes who were better all along started realizing they could play, too, and it got more competitive."

"The games are a lot more physical now," Sue says. "Dirty play still gets penalized, but the refs let a whole lot more happen before they'll call it. There are all kinds of cheap shots that go by."

"I can usually let it go," Alicia says. "But every once in a while I really feel it building up inside of me. If someone does something that's really stupid, you just wanna go and really let them have it."

"A couple of weeks ago there was this girl," Sue says. "She was using her stick all over the place. Three times she got me—a trip, a hook, a spear—and the ref didn't call any of it. Then, later on, we were digging for the puck at centre ice and I caught her skate with my stick. She went down, and right away she was screaming at me: 'I'm going to kill you!' she was saying. 'I'm going to take you out to the parking lot and kill you.' I couldn't believe anyone would say that, but she kept saying it, like she really meant it, and the ref was right there. He just laughed.

"The women refs won't let it get that far. They know that it can really get out of hand, but the male refs think it's funny.

"I'm not proud of what I did about it, either. There were just seventeen seconds left on the clock; she came across the blue line and I pounded her. I really dropped her. I felt ashamed, because it was a cowardly thing to do.

I don't think of myself as that kind of player, but I was obviously still really angry inside, and it just came out.

"The things you see on a rink, I sometimes I think it's a kind of road rage. It's like people turn into someone else when they get in that environment, and the rules they follow everywhere else just get thrown out the window. I feel it in myself. If I'm pushed, I'll get to a place I really don't want to go."

I ask her where she first learned to play.

"My parents divorced when I was eight years old. Mum wanted to give me something else to think about while things were so crazy, I guess. I said I wanted to play hockey, so she signed me up.

"It was the Scarborough girls' hockey league in 1978. She got this beat-up, used equipment for me because she was sure it wouldn't last, that I would get bored and quit after the first season, but that was twenty-six years ago. I haven't missed a season since.

"Mum was so supportive. She came to every one of my games right through until my late teens, and even into my twenties. She's still my number one fan, and she was right. It really did deflect a lot of what was going on at home."

I ask about her father. Did he ever coach or play?

"He left when I was pretty young," she says. "I didn't really get to know him very well. He's never seen me play."

She paused a moment, looking away.

"He hurt my Mum a lot. There was a lot of physical stuff between them, and my sister and I saw some really bad stuff. It still really hurts to think about it.

"We communicated by letter at first. I didn't want him to phone the house in case Mum answered and she would have to hear his voice, so he would write me letters when he first left. We had the every-other-weekend thing, too, but after a while I really just couldn't stand the tension between them when he came to pick me up at the door. It was just too painful. I had to distance myself. I just kind of brushed him aside.

"Mum's got Alzheimer's now. She's in hospital, and losing memories all the time. There are so many things I still don't know. That's why I'm thinking about Dad. He's in his late seventies now. Time's running out.

"I saw him a couple of years ago, and he said he was sorry. I can't forget all the stuff that happened between him and Mum, but there are so many things I still want to know. I think about it every day. I don't want to grow old full of regrets.

"How did you and Todd meet?" I ask as she's pulling on her jacket.

"At a coed tournament," she says with a smile. "It's going to be tough if our kids don't want to play."

• • •

Late January brings the select team's first out-of-town tournament, in Niagara Falls, New York: three days of mini-stick hockey in the hotel hallways, leaden breakfasts in an apparently infinite number of Denny's restaurants, and the inspired pranks of eleven-year-old boys, most notably peeing on the rocks in the hotel sauna.

Between pranks there are hockey games against teams that make us wonder what, exactly, they put in the eggs at Denny's. These boys are huge, some of them alarmingly so. Dave had warned us there was a very good chance we'd be outgunned here, but even he is surprised. We come away with one win, and in retrospect, it's hard to know how we managed even that.

It's also hard to know how we got out of Niagara Falls without any injuries. Hitting is becoming more and more a part of the select team's games, and the hits are getting hard.

Last week they faced the team from Don Mills, and the outcome turned not so much on hitting, but on the lack of it.

Don Mills has emerged as this year's arch-rival—especially for Wesley, Derek, Ben and Andrew, because they are in the same sixth-grade class as Matthew, Patrick, Ben and Sam, who all play for Don Mills. Every game the two teams play brings schoolyard fallout for weeks.

Late in the third period of last week's game, the Don Mills captain took the puck from one end of the ice to the other, weaving around all five Leaside players, and finished the rush by tucking the tying goal neatly between our goalie's pads.

Leaside had been outskating, outpassing and outhustling Don Mills all night long, but they gave it away in that one, ten-second rush.

"All you have to do is just step into the guy," Roman said at practice that weekend. "That's all it takes. Just step in his way and push him off the puck. That's part of the game now. You have to think that way, or those guys are going to just waltz through every time."

Tonight we are playing York Mills, a team well above us in the standings. They beat us by five goals the last time we met. They are a big team and they know it. It is one of the strange sights in minor hockey to see rosy-cheeked kids who could have stepped out of a TV situation comedy, begging Dad for a Slushie after the game, when mere minutes earlier they were brutes on the ice, literally throwing themselves at each other with the dark intensity of veteran thugs.

The Leaside team is playing effectively, skating and passing well, but it isn't doing them much good. They are simply getting blown off the puck with every hit. On defence, Taylor is absorbing check after check. Patrick, in goal, barely has time to breathe between shots. By the end of the first period we are down by two goals and it is clear that if we want room to move on the ice in this game, we are going to have to start checking back.

It turns on one hit. Andrew is coming up the wing. A York Mills player lines him up, expecting an easy check, when Andrew passes the puck a few seconds early and uses all of his momentum to plaster the kid to the ice. It's a lesson in Newtonian physics—force equals mass times acceleration. The kid is stunned at first, then humiliated, and immediately after that, livid. He swings his stick at Andrew and just misses catching him on the unprotected back of his calf. Andrew has no idea, but the Leaside bench sees it, and the message is very clear. These kids have been intimidating smaller teams all year long, and they've gotten used to the idea that no one is going to give it back.

A surge of anger and ambition washes through our team, and the stakes rise very quickly. The York Mills players are giving up the puck with every hit, but they're also looking for every opportunity to hit back and are getting reckless in the process.

Hitting works in hockey. It knocks the other player off balance, both literally and emotionally. When players start thinking about getting even or not getting hit again, they're no longer thinking about skating and passing and scoring goals. Great passes begin at a level of creative imagination that is barely conscious. If the mind is fixating on fury, or terror, or both, it's disabled.

The Leaside team learns this lesson from both sides, but it's the player who stays focused on his own radar who pays the highest price.

York Mills is ahead 2–1 in the second period when Wesley's line comes on. They move the puck well, from Evan to Wesley and over to Nathan next to the boards. He carries the puck across the blue line as he draws the defenceman towards him and sees Wesley a short pass away, heading for the net.

What Nathan doesn't see is the York Mills winger speeding in from behind.

Nathan waits until the defenceman is committed to hitting him before he releases the pass. It gives the charging winger all the time he needs. The defenceman stands Nathan up from the front while the winger drives an elbow into the back of his head, sending him hard into the boards.

Nathan falls in a heap to the ice.

The parents gasp. The bench roars—me among them—and Wesley, to my surprise, charges the York Mills winger and hammers him into the boards. It is an entirely impulsive reaction, and one I've never seen from him. He is furious.

The referees stop the play. Brad, our team trainer, and Dave trot across the ice. The rink falls silent.

The ref signals a penalty and sends the winger off the ice. Hitting from behind is a five-minute major, plus an immediate two-game suspension for the offending player. There is a ripple through the crowd over this, complaints of injustice from one group of parents and murmurs of quiet satisfaction from the other.

It is an otherworldly moment. If any of these parents, including me, were to witness any other situation where an eleven-year-old boy is hit in the head so hard that he crumples to the ground, we would run to help with nothing in mind but the child's safety. Here, though, even as Nathan lies motionless, a good number of parents are still disputing whether it was really a hit from behind.

After a few minutes Dave and Brad help a very woozy-looking Nathan to his feet and walk him back to the bench. They are each holding an elbow and he clearly needs their support.

Nathan is back in the game by the third period, although the sense of fear and anger is palpable from the entire Leaside group—parents and players—anytime anyone gets near him. There are no more incidents that night. Leaside scores on the power play that follows the hit on Nathan, and the game ends in a tie.

The players are in the lobby after the game, lined up at the concession stand for Slushies and drinks, looking like kids once again. The parents talk in low voices amongst themselves, eyeing the opposing parents with just the slightest unease as we all merge on the way through the main doors and out into the parking lot. Some might be looking for the kid who got hurt, some for the kid who hurt him, but no one says anything, and we all climb into our cars and head home for the night.

• • •

The soft hands and hard hits of Todd Bertuzzi have become front-page news.

It has been a great season for Bertuzzi. His Vancouver Canucks are winning and the sports pages have been pre-dicting a long-deserved Stanley Cup. Most are crediting the team's success to the combination of their high-scor-ing captain, Markus Naslund, and Bertuzzi's tremendous intensity. He has emerged as the day's great example of the power forward—a skilled player who can hit.

As of this week, though, Bertuzzi's name is famous for something else.

Three weeks ago, in mid-February, the Canucks were playing the Colorado Avalanche. Steve Moore, an Avalanche rookie, was out of position, and in trying to cover his mistake he caught Naslund with a questionable open-ice hit. There was no penalty called on the play, but Moore's shoulder hit Naslund in the head. The Canucks captain suffered a concussion and needed thirteen stitches across his forehead and face.

Two nights ago, the two teams played again, and it wasn't a good game for Vancouver. By the third period, Colorado had a six-goal lead. The next time Steve Moore took the ice, Bertuzzi came out as well, and he was looking for revenge. He challenged Moore to a fight, but Moore skated away. Bertuzzi followed him the length of the ice, eventually grabbing Moore's jersey from behind and driving all of his two hundred and forty-five pounds into a punch that hit Moore at the base of the skull and then drove his head face-first into the ice.

Moore's neck was broken in three places. There is wide speculation that he will never play hockey again. A tearful Bertuzzi held a press conference this afternoon. "Steve," he said, "I just want to apologize for what happened out there. I had no intention of hurting you and I feel awful for what transpired. . . . To the fans of hockey and the fans of Vancouver, to the kids that watch this game, I'm truly sorry. I don't play the game that way. I'm not a mean-spirited person. I'm sorry for what happened."

His remorse was convincing, and it is hard to reconcile the shaken man in the nice suit with the brutal thug whose cowardly attack has been played and replayed on television all day long.

There are other factors in the story. This game was not the first time the two teams had met since Naslund's injury. They played another game just last week, and Bertuzzi and Moore were even on the ice at the same time, but that game ended in a tie. With both clubs in very close contention late in the season, Bertuzzi clearly wasn't willing to take a major penalty in a game his team could win. So, he boxed up his rage until it was more convenient to let it out.

The NHL has temporarily suspended Bertuzzi, and will announce a final punishment shortly. Meanwhile, the Vancouver Police have talked of laying assault charges.

## XI

"KEEP IT AWAY FROM YOURSELF a little more," Dave Trombley says, pulling my stick away from my body. "Get the butt end away from your chest so you can move. Give yourself some room." And he demonstrates by slaloming his stick through a line of pylons as he glides over top, one skate on either side of the line, the shaft of his stick swinging easily around as the blade darts between them like a weaver's shuttle.

"You see?" he asks. "Try it again."

It is strange. I have grown used to the idea that I need to hang onto my stick with all I've got just to get through the play, but these pylons are very close together. There isn't time to think about it, and if I'm holding my stick too hard I can't move it fast enough. I take a few strides, try to keep my stick held away from my chest, start to weave and I'm through. I haven't knocked any pylons over.

There are three of us here today, and the general idea is to get more done with less effort.

"Receive the puck," Dave says, as he and Gary pass back and forth. The passes are fast and crisp, but the puck never bounces away. Dave cradles it as if he were handling a lacrosse stick, and the puck acts as if there is a basket there, too.

"Keep the hands loose, and let the stick move *with* the puck. You're not fighting to control it, you just want it to go where you're going. If it's already moving that way, let it take you there."

Gary and I are paired off for this passing drill, and we move up and down the ice, the puck leading the way. It is better.

Dave starts us on a new drill. Two of us stand at the opposite ends of the blue line, with the third deep along the boards. We are three corners of a square. The teacher is in the middle, and our job is to keep him from getting the puck. We do that by passing and by moving to the open corner. It's a simple concept, but it takes real concentration. When one student has the puck, he has about two seconds while the teacher is rushing him to decide which of the other two students he will pass to. During that two seconds, someone has to move to the open corner to provide a clear target.

For a few minutes we are in disarray, and Dave gets the puck every time. When I receive a pass, I have the panicky response that I know so well—I want to get rid of it as quickly as I can. But this is not a game, and instead of five or six bungled passes in three periods of hockey, the passes are coming every few beats. When I screw up, I get another chance, and another. It is fast and exhilarating, and after thirty or forty passes I begin to see that two seconds can be a very long time. Gary, I notice, is looking not just at me when I have the puck, but at each of us in turn, all the time. I try to do the same and I find I can anticipate what the others will do, and win myself an extra second—a fifty-per-cent increase.

"That's it!" Dave calls out as I send the puck a full second ahead of him to Gary, who is waiting across the blue line. "Think slowly, act fast! Good!"

We are laughing now and connecting passes all the faster, and Dave is working harder and laughing, too. When a player of Dave's calibre can have this much fun while giving us so much information, something is going very much the way it should.

He has a few minutes before his next student arrives, so I ask him about himself.

"I started hockey when I was four, at Scarborough Gardens Arena," he tells me. "Jim Crawford put together forty of us kids from four to six years old, and over the following two years we practised two times a week, focused on individual skill development. Then he took the top fifteen kids, and I was one of them. Our team was the Scarborough Super Sabres. When we played in house league the average score was 20–0. We were the only kids who could raise the puck, who could pass, who had positional playing. It was the foundation for everything I learned as a player and everything I now do as a teacher.

"I guess the only thing that was hard for me in hockey was that I was small. I had speed and hockey sense and I had the hands, but I wasn't big enough for 'AAA.' So, after pee wee I went down to 'AA,' and that's where I learned how to play my game. The age group above called me up for every game that year. I was the leading scorer in both age groups. The older team won the Ontario championship that year. I got five points in the all-star game, and things started to fall into place.

"I went back up to AAA and I had 120 points in my last year in midget, but I heard it again and again—'Put on weight.' You get to the point that you're sick of eating. I was eating six full courses a meal, but I just couldn't put on any more weight.

"In 1991 I graduated from Clarkson University in New York with a 3.0 grade point average. I was in the top five in scoring in the NCAA, and that June I was drafted second overall in the supplemental draft by the Quebec Nordiques.

"Training camp was fantastic. You have people taking care of you. If you need a stick—done. Fix my helmet—done. They brought seventy-two guys to camp and cut thirty the first week, and the next week another ten. It wasn't until October that the last few of us got sent down to the American Hockey League.

"I was ready for that. The other centres on that team were Joe Sakic, Mats Sundin and Claude Lapointe. After three weeks of playing with those guys I had done well. I ended up with the New Haven Nighthawks, in Connecticut.

"I played four games in New Haven, and then, on October 21—it was a Sunday—we were making a television commercial to promote the team. I was in front of the net, and as I turned to go and get the puck I ran into the defenceman and I got a tingling all through my body. I fell down on the ice. I'd lost all feeling and couldn't move at all for a couple of minutes before the feeling came back to my lower extremities, but I still had pins and needles all over.

"I took a shower and got changed and went back to the hotel, but it was still driving me nuts, so I took myself to the hospital and this old doctor took some x-rays, but he told me there was nothing wrong, that I was fine. I wasn't fine. I could hardly sleep.

"The next morning I went to emergency and it was like the red light went on. They strapped me into a gurney and I spent six hours staring at the ceiling. They gave me an MRI and they found it: a narrowing of the spinal column where the spinal cord sits—it's called spinal stenosis. For most people, the tube in their spine that holds their spinal cord measures fifteen to seventeen millimetres in diameter. Mine is twelve. It puts me at a much higher risk for a spinal-cord injury.

"That's what happened on the ice. A disk just moved over a little and nudged my spinal cord. It kind of bruised it; that's why I had all the tingling, and that's why it shut down and then rebooted itself two minutes later.

"The doctor who did the MRI came out. 'You better find a new line of work,' he said. I went for another opinion. I saw eleven more specialists—in Boston, Dallas, Toronto. Twelve spinal specialists that were among the best in the world, and six of them told me to go back and play; the other six said to stop right away. These doctors were at both extremes, and I was in the middle, but there *is* no middle with a spinal injury.

"All of that testing took two years, and in that time I started coaching. I helped out with my neighbour's son's team. The parents were telling me that I was good, that I could communicate how the game worked. The next time I went for testing at Toronto Western Hospital, the spinal specialist was there with five interns, and they were still arguing about what I should do. I decided that if I was that hard to make a decision about, then the decision was 'no.'

"I'd had two years to get used to the idea of life after hockey, but it was still rough. I was watching guys on TV that I'd just been playing with, and they were living the boyhood dream that I had worked for all my life. I *did* make it. I got drafted. I signed a contract. I skated with those players . . .

"Things happen for a reason. When I look at it now I think it was a blessing from God saying, 'You know what? You've been pushing yourself in your little frame and this is as far as I'm going to let you go.'"

"So," I asked Dave, "if you see a smaller kid coming to you, and he's hearing that he's too little to play, what do you tell him?"

"Whether they're six foot two or really small, I will never take away that boyhood dream. Boyhood dreams only last for a very short time, and all of a sudden you hit the real world. But while you're trying to make a boyhood dream come true you still go to school, you still learn about being good to people. In a boyhood dream you can still obtain all your life skills and become a quality person. Why give up that?"

*   *   *

The Vultures are in deep. It's the third period. We are down two goals and it's hard to imagine things improving.

I should be off the ice. I've been on for at least two minutes and I'm too tired to be of any use at all, but we're stuck in our own end and I just can't get to the bench. The guys waiting to go on are yelling at us to get a whistle. Don, at centre, is yelling at me to stay up by the blue line and guard the other team's defenceman, and Bruce, our goalie, is yelling at everybody.

All game long I've been looking for a chance to use my new passing skills, my skating skills, or maybe even to show how much my shot has improved—to turn the game around in one spectacular moment. I wait, I look, I think. I know there is a great play somewhere around me, but time and time again I simply can't see it, and I end up losing the puck.

I manage to get myself back out to the blue line and away from the clamour around the net. I'm thinking of just heading for the bench no matter how dangerous it is, when Daryl takes a wild swing at the puck and it bounces my way.

The other team's defenceman is on me. We jostle against the boards and in my desperation, just for a moment, I see I've got control.

I begin to look for the big pass again, but through my exhaustion another more manageable idea comes along.

I don't have to save this game. I've spent the previous two periods making it painfully obvious that I have no hope of doing that, anyway. I just have to make things a little less horrible. If I can make things just slightly less embarrassing for us, just raise our lowest level a tiny bit, then I'll have something to feel good about later on, and that'll be a whole lot better than what I've got now.

Chris is tearing up the far wing. If I can get him the puck he'll be home free and probably score. And then we can score again and maybe even win.

On the other hand, Daryl is just behind me. He's waiting and watching and nobody's on him. He's only a few feet away and not even out of the zone yet, but it's a short pass I can accomplish. It's something I can actually do.

It works.

Daryl makes the pass to Chris. Chris charges in alone and sends in a blistering wrist shot and . . . Well, that's all. The truth is, the shot isn't really all that blistering, and the goalie makes an easy save. We're still losing, but we've earned the chance to get to the bench, at least, and given the next line a face-off in the other team's zone.

It's a step.

Ten minutes later, we lose the game anyway, but not before Noel scores and brings us just one goal away. We pull Bruce for the last thirty seconds, and although we don't manage any real chances to tie it up, as we're going back to the dressing room the talk is a lot more boisterous than it might have been otherwise, and it's clear we are going home happier than we were when we arrived.

Fifteen minutes later, we're piled into Aladdin's Palace and I'm sitting across from Noel.

He is a bit of a mystery to me. He is a terrific hockey player, and more than once I've asked myself what he is doing down here in the "D" league with us. Dozens of better teams would welcome him in an instant. He is very approachable, but ever since I found out he is Steve Thomas's little brother I've been reluctant to invade his privacy and ask him about it.

There are still things I want to know, though, so I swallow my worries and ask.

"There are pros and cons." he tells me. "The pros are that I've met all kinds of people and they have treated me very, very well, even though they may not have had any idea what I was really like.

"Steve is six years older than me. I played hockey all through my childhood, starting at age five. Ours was a very sports-minded family. My father played competitive soccer where he grew up in England until he was twenty years old, and both my older brothers, Robin and Steve, played hockey seriously as well.

"Dad never coached us, but he was very attentive. After the game he would explain what he felt could have been better. He was a quiet person, but we'd still hear him in the stands. 'Skate, skate!' he'd call, always pushing us to do our best, but never to a negative point.

"Steve was the most like Dad, just full of determination. It was something he always had in him to go and get what he wanted.

"It's overwhelming when your brother makes the NHL. Your whole family becomes a celebrity of a kind and people start looking at you very differently. 'What about you?' they'd ask. 'How come you can't play the way *he* can?'"

Noel took a drink of his beer and looked away a moment.

"After midget, when I was sixteen, I had a decision to make. The competitive level really wasn't working for me anymore. Coaches and parents expected so much. It was like they expected me to be Steve, and when I wasn't I'd let them down. So I quit playing at that level, and I had the choice of playing non-competitive juvenile hockey or taking a break. I decided to take a break.

"The only hard part was not playing with my buddies anymore. I got my licence and enjoyed the rest of my teenage years. If you're going to be a hockey player, you have to give that up—you have to give up weekends at the cottage and goofing around with your pals. It's like you become a kind of adult right away. That didn't happen to me.

"I joined a men's league when I was twenty-five, but it really wasn't fun. I didn't tell a soul who I was, but somehow they found out, and when I came out for my very first game they had my sweater ready for me. They'd chosen team colours that were just like the Chicago Blackhawks, because that's where Steve was playing. They gave me number 32, just like Steve, without even asking, and we had our names across the back, so mine said 'Thomas.' They even made me assistant captain, because that's what Steve was.

"I guess at that age a lot of the guys think maybe they still have a chance at that NHL dream. These guys kept track of their stats and they got in fights in the dressing room over who'd get to take home the game sheet. They just had too much to prove. I'd given up on that dream a decade ago.

"So I stayed away from hockey until this year. I figure at age thirty-four, most of us have gotten over that stuff. I only have one reason for being here now—because it's fun. It's been twenty years since I gave up on expecting anything more, and I'm not sure there really is anything better, anyway."

• • •

Wesley and I have been talking about tonight's game for days.

In practice, Dave and Roman have drilled the team on puck control, on passing, on backchecking and positional play. Dave Trombley has been reinforcing all of that in his early-morning sessions. In our talks before and after the last couple of games, Dave, Roman and I have been sending home the same message: play with intensity, don't be afraid to play the body, come off the ice with absolutely nothing left inside. Once the puck drops tonight, there won't be anything let to save it for.

After last year's frustrating experience, everyone is ready for this year's playoff games to go the other way. This season has been considerably more successful. The team has won more games, finished up a tier in the standings, and the improvements the players have been working on since October have really started to settle in. Now it's time to prove it.

This is the first of a two-game playoff series against the team Leaside most wants to beat but hasn't yet: Don Mills.

After the two tied games earlier in the season, Don Mills and Leaside met again in a tournament held at the Leaside Arena. Despite the partisan crowd and the blaring music between plays and the feeling that we honestly are the better team, we lost by a score of 2–1.

The schoolyard rhetoric has been building ever since, and when the regular season wound up with Leaside and Don Mills slated for the opening round of the playoffs, the players on both teams cheered at the prospect.

Wesley is all but silent in the back seat as we arrive at the rink. He is breathing evenly, his eyes shut in concentration. He finds a spot on the bench in the dressing room and says nothing while dressing, and as Dave makes his pregame address the entire team sits motionless, heads down, waiting.

The players stretch, skate their drills and take their places on the bench as if in a vacuum, still almost soundless, even and controlled.

They glide to centre ice for the face-off. The referee holds the puck over Wesley and the Don Mills centre's sticks, and as it leaves his hand, the bench, the fans and the entire arena seems to hold its breath.

Then the puck lands and all of that energy explodes outward.

Leaside is on fire. Nathan has kept a spot in the lineup, and he and Wesley have their radar on full. Devlin, back from his knee injury since mid-February, is at his fiery, charging best. Patrick is imposing and solid in the net and Taylor and the rest of the defence corps play tough and smart through two entire periods.

Still, the teams are very evenly matched. Leaside is dominating the play, spending shift after shift exclusively in the opposing zone, but the Don Mills goalie is having a great game. He is huge, for one thing—there isn't very much room for our shooters. He is also very quick, and he seems to have luck on his side. Pucks clang off the crossbar. Point shots rifle in and just miss the open side. Rebounds bounce away, but never to a waiting stick.

Our players are doing everything we asked. They are moving the puck, they are skating hard both ways, they are playing with intensity and finishing each shift as if it is their last, but by the early minutes of the third period the game is tied at one goal apiece.

Then the unthinkable happens again. A Don Mills player intercepts a pass in the neutral zone and turns sharply towards our net. The forwards are all charging in the wrong direction. Taylor, on defence, so strong now and so willing to step in front of the player and do what so desperately needs to be done, is caught by surprise and never has a chance. The lapse lasts no more than two or three seconds, but in that time the Don Mills player waltzes in alone and finds an open corner. There are six minutes left.

The three forward lines will get two shifts each at most in the time that remains. Wesley plays his heart out—digging in the corners, pouncing on loose pucks, backchecking with all he can muster—but the minutes tick away with no change in the score.

With less than two minutes to go, Dave sends Wesley's line out again. He wins the puck near centre ice and turns for the Don Mills zone with Nathan trailing behind. I lean on the boards with my hands tucked into my chest, saying "yes, yes, yes" under my breath, willing the puck forward, willing my son to do what I know he can do so well, when there is a sudden whack against the boards beside me.

It is Charlie, who has been on the ice for his shift and wants to come off. In the milliseconds that slip by, and as I crank open the gate, a tiny question mark appears in my mind. Charlie stands aside. Devin, the next winger, steps up to the gate. My hand is on his back, and as I watch Devin's skates stepping out onto the ice, the question mark pops.

"No!" my mind is shrieking, but it is too late.

It isn't always the case, but in some rinks the forward gate on the bench is actually inside the blue line. By stepping on the ice when he does, at my request, Devin has automatically crossed the blue line before the puck. He is offside.

The play is whistled down, and Wesley's hard-earned opportunity is gone. We pull the goalie, and keep play in the Don Mills zone for the final forty seconds, but to no avail. The buzzer sounds and Don Mills has won. Our team has played the game of the season for three full periods minus one two- or three-second lapse.

The dressing room is silent now, again, but it is nothing like the silence that rested here before. It is one day before March break, and although we don't yet know when the second game of this playoff series will be, the chances are very good that it will come some time in the next seven days, and if that is the case, the team will be an entirely different one than was playing here tonight.

Dave is upbeat in his postgame talk. They should leave with their heads held high, he tells them, and they do. In fact, by the time they are changed and packed up to go, they are what they always are at the end of a game, no matter how it went: they are kids. They bean each other with snowballs. They laugh and wrestle and roar. The heartbreak of the evening is, by the look of it, barely a heartbreak at all.

I am watching Wesley. I am still picturing the moment that almost was. I can still feel what he should have been able to do, and what I should have done to make it happen for him.

He and Melissa are with their mother tonight, and for the rest of March break. They will be going away for the week. The chances are very good that the Leaside select hockey season is over, and whatever hopes I had of sharing a victory with Wesley as his coach are gone.

Melissa is here, and as I hug her I am surprised at the rush of emotion. I love these children so much, and I realize as Wesley comes over to say goodbye that nothing in that love has been changed by the end of my marriage. This raging grip always been there all along and always will.

I want to share that with them, but it is none of their business. Their business is to be children. My business is to create the kind of life for them that allows them to do that, no matter how little of their time with me that will mean.

I go to my car. I sit in the darkness and see my children loading their things into their mother's car and hesitating by the open door. Melissa, who came to watch her brother play, is looking around the parking lot. She is looking for me, to wave goodbye, but there is no escaping the truth of this moment, or the next, or the one after that.

They are going to spend two-thirds of the rest of their childhoods without me. Two-thirds of the mornings, two-thirds of the meals, two-thirds of the arguments, two-thirds of the heartbreaks, two-thirds of the time with nothing at all to do but sit together and think of nothing to say.

Two-thirds of everything, and nothing I can come up with will change that—no joke, no subway game, no wrong-side crossover, no rising wrist shot, no tape-to-tape cross-ice pass that finds Wesley streaming in on the net all alone and scoring the winning goal. Nothing can ever bring back what we have lost.

I'm not sure why I ever thought it could.

**XII**

THE SELECT TEAM'S SECOND PLAYOFF game falls in the middle of March break. Six of the team's regular skaters are there. Dave fills what other spots he can with kids from the age group below. Leaside loses by a score of 4–0.

The select season is over.

The team ordered jackets for the coaches this year, and I have one. It's black, with the red and gold Leaside Flames logo on the chest, and the word "Coach" embroidered in gold, cursive letters on the sleeve. It's the kind of thing I would have laughed at twenty years ago, but I have worn this jacket every day since I got it. I don't even think about it anymore. It's just my jacket.

I thought about it today, though, as I left for work, especially seeing the word "Coach" on the sleeve.

I've noticed, as I look back on what I've written through these pages, that some of the time I refer to the Leaside team as "them" and sometimes as "us." I've been reluctant to choose which it really ought to be, but I'm still wearing the jacket, so it's clearly more one than the other.

Our season is over.

Wesley called me tonight from his ski holiday with his mother, and I had the unpleasant task of telling him what happened. He was disappointed, but not surprised. He spent most of the call talking about how much fun he's been having.

I tell him to enjoy the rest of the week. He says he will.

• • •

That's one.

Back to the red line, turn hard and sprint, over the blue line, take the puck wide, pass to the target—there.

That's two, and it's back to the red line again.

I'm practising at New Centre Ice. I've got a puck set up in the slot as a marker for Don, and another one on the far goalpost as a marker for Chris. I'm carrying the puck from centre ice to the corner, choosing a marker, and making the pass—or, on every third run, coming in on the net myself and taking a shot. It's three o'clock in the afternoon on a Wednesday. I'm the only one here. I paid my five bucks an hour ago. I've got plenty of energy left.

The last time I skated here was my Sunday-night game with the Vultures—our first playoff game.

We lost.

The things I remember most, though, have nothing to do with who won. Early in the game, the opposing winger tripped me. We were at centre ice, and the ref wasn't looking. I was charging along the boards. He stuck his blade in my skates, and I went down like a bag of bricks.

I swore at him and chipped at him with my stick. We spent the rest of the shift jostling and shoving, near the puck or not, and when the play was whistled down and we were both heading back to the bench, he clunked me with an elbow and I shoved him back.

"Bastard," I said.

Then, the next time we were out, and waiting for the face-off, I glared at him sideways and muttered through my teeth, "Don't trip me this time." As I was saying it, though, I somehow heard the sound of my own voice like that of a schoolyard kid complaining to the teacher, and I couldn't help but smile. Here we were, two forty-some-thing men all decked out in our tons of plastic armour, facing off like gladiators fighting to the death, and what comes out of my mouth is the adult equivalent of "Nana-nana-boo-boo."

He smirked, too, and we both broke up laughing.

Then the puck dropped and the game was on.

I looked for him when we shook hands, and that gave us another laugh.

We're playing again on Sunday, and I'm really looking forward to it—to playing and digging as hard as I can, and to seeing that winger again, even though the last game was a chippy one, and this week's will almost certainly be more that way. I still want to play.

• • •

The Leaside house-league championship game comes as a kind of bonus at the end of the season. The select team's loss was so hard and so sudden that it was easy to think hockey was gone for the year, but it isn't.

There are five house-league teams, and the select players are evenly spread out among them. So the same group of kids gets to face off again, but this time against each other, and the challenge is very real.

Wesley's team is up against a group that includes four excellent select players, and there is a sweetness in the matchup. One of those four is the redoubtable Patrick, the goalie, and another is the player who knows Wesley's tricks better than he knows them himself, Nathan.

Nathan's team dominates the play, but through it all a new star emerges: the goalie who was one off the alternate list in the fall and who has been coming to the early-morning practices all year, Scott. He plays a spectacular game, and by the middle of the third period, mirroring the Don Mills game only two weeks before, the score is tied at one goal apiece.

Then, with two minutes left, Wesley picks up a loose puck in the neutral zone and finds an opening between the defencemen. Patrick makes the save, but Wesley collects the rebound and finally finds an open corner.

He raises his stick and throws back his head. The score stays as it is, and his becomes the winning goal. After such a good year, when he has played so well so many times, this is the way his hockey story really ought to end, with the right kid doing the right thing when he needs to, and his celebration is as well earned as it could be.

I know it's the way this season ought to end, because I can see it clearly from here. I'm up in the stands, cheering and waving, and he is down there, on the ice, in the game.

• • •

The very next day, it's my turn.

The game is set for eight o'clock, and we, the Vultures, arrive early. We're realists, though, because as we're dressing the talk turns to the season that will begin again in a month or so.

"Hey," Joe says, interrupting when Brock and Daryl ask the group if we want to stay with New Centre Ice for the summer. "What's going on? You guys already deciding this'll be our last game?"

"Well," Brock says, and Bruce, who is dressed, clumps past Joe to the door and out to the rink.

Joe watches him go and turns back to us.

"Seriously," he says. "What if we win?"

No one answers.

It's a two-game series, and we've already lost one. In order to stay alive, we first need to win this game to tie the series, and then to score the first goal in the sudden-death overtime period that immediately follows. That period lasts all of five minutes, and if that doesn't find a winner, we're into penalty shots. It is a brutal way to decide a game, but two more teams are scheduled to play at nine o'clock, and another two after that.

It's a business.

My legs are buzzing as we line up for the face-off, but when the puck drops, for a moment, the play is suddenly clear. Don wins the draw and passes to Chris. He carries it across the blue line and shoots. It bounces to me and I take a shot, then another, and it's in the net. I can see it there, inside the mesh. The game is twenty seconds old. I scored.

The goal, certainly not something that any of us would have predicted, has a galvanizing effect. We're playing our best. The other guys still have plenty of life in them, though, and there is one pesky winger who is fast and dirty, hacking and hooking and poking anything and anyone in his way. He is carefully gauging what this referee will consider a step over the line, and he comes as close as he can to that, especially when he's close to our goalie, Bruce.

It works. After one flurry in front of the net, Bruce loses his cool and knocks the winger down. The ref issues him a penalty for interference. Bruce yells at the ref for that, and he gives us another penalty. We are two men short now, and Bruce is still yelling at the ref, while we start yelling at *him*—mostly two words: "shut" and "up."

Brock, Daryl and Cliff hold off the other team for most of the penalty, but not all of it. The pesky winger scores to tie the game and does a little hot-dogging for Bruce's benefit in the process.

"Hey," Big Joe calls to the winger when the play is stopped and they're heading to the bench, "look at this." And he points to the back of his leg. Joe's sock is worn. There is a series of dirty-grey slashes across his calf.

"See that?" Joe says. "You don't want to mess with him. He's crazy. He's been slashing me all season, and I'm on *his* team."

"Really?" the winger asks.

"Uh-huh," Joe says. "Take it from me." And he skates to the bench, while the winger watches him go, looking again at the back of his leg.

The winger isn't much of a factor after that.

But the game is not over. Don scores in the second, and they even it up. Then, with ten minutes left, Noel uncorks a blinding slap shot from the point that breaks the sound barrier before it just about rips through the net, and we are winning 3–2.

Late in the third, I get the puck at centre.

There is a skating drill I've been doing off and on since I learned it from Dave Picton last year. It comes to me as I cross the blue line, a zig-zag pattern of left and right crossovers, and before I know what's happened I'm around the defence and bearing in on the goalie.

I wind up for the shot, but as I'm releasing I feel a jolt of pain and I'm flat on my back. The defenceman I just got around took a two-handed chop with his stick, like he was splitting wood with an axe. The blow glanced off my helmet and landed on my shoulder with so much force it knocked me off my feet. The ref sends him off for the rest of the game, and we hang on to win, tying the series.

Three minutes later, on an assist from Chris, Don scores in overtime, and we've won.

"The Vultures live to pick another corpse," Johnny says as we troop from the ice.

Our reward is a semifinal berth one week later, against the team that finished in first place. We play well, but this time it is not our night. When we leave Aladdin's Palace in the early-morning hours, all that's left of the Vultures' first season are the memories, the bragging and a glow that lasts for months to come.

There's also a scar.

When I took off my gear after our first-round playoff victory, I was amazed to see that I was bleeding all over the inside of my shoulder pads. The defenceman's two-handed chop had been strong enough to break the skin and leave a gash, even though it had to get through two layers of armour to do it.

We shook hands after that game. I saw the winger I'd laughed with, and although I don't remember seeing the hacking defenceman's face, I know I shook his hand, too, because I shook them all. I held no grudge. I said the same thing to each player as I did, and each time I heard the same thing back.

"Good game," we all said, and we meant it.

· · ·

One bright summer morning in May, I get a call from Heather Gill.

They are still playing shinny on Saturday nights, but they're short this week. Am I interested?

"Well," I say, "Wesley's with me this weekend. Have you got room for two?"

The older players praise Wesley; the younger ones, like Jeff Gill, remind him not to coast; and Sue, as they go into the corner, steals the puck from him and drops him on his butt.

"Hey!" he calls, as she chuckles away towards the net.

When he returns the favour on the next shift, both benches stand and cheer.

Then, somewhere around the midway point, Kevin passes to me on the wing, I charge up the boards, crossing over as I go, and get around the defence. I'm looking to the net and trying to decide if I can turn hard enough for a shot when I hear the on-ice call I've longed to hear for months.

"Dad!"

He's in the slot. It's an easy backhand. Tape-to-tape, and when it works, I simply can't help myself. I stop where I am and watch as he skates in alone and lets go a rising wrist shot to the top right-hand corner.

Al stops it.

It doesn't matter.

Lori Gemmell

**THE VULTURES**

*Front:* Guy Perry, Steve Easton (lying down), Noel Thomas, Jonathan Mingay, me, Blair Hogg.
*Back:* Eric Van Wolde, Kevin Ely, Daryl Jackson, Dave Allaway, Chris Maxwell, Val Gigante, Brock Smith
*Missing and former team members:* Dave Kinnear, Joseph McLuckie, Mike Muise, Don Pecora, Bruce Bullock, Andre Cleghorn, Cliff Good, Dave Gort, Chris Maxwell, Les Nip, Cam "Bubbles" Stewart and Terece Tai.

*Note the time on the scoreboard—that's 12:46 a.m. All in a day's work.*

# WESLEY WEIGHS IN

HOCKEY IS MY FAVOURITE THING to do and I can't imagine life without it. Sometimes during a long break between games, when it feels like ages since I've played, I get a craving that won't go away until I fulfill it. Hockey gives me a feeling of power. It's an exhilaration I get when I'm skating down the right side at top speed, or taking a wrist shot that goes exactly where I want it to go. That exhilaration is unmatched to me so far.

Having my dad as a coach has been a great advantage at times, and also a handicap. I'll start with the hard part. It's dangerous to get family life mixed up with hockey. I feel more comfortable arguing with him than any other coach. That gets me angry and can disrupt my game. Also, it must be difficult for my father, because if I were to get hit in a dirty way he might react more than he would if, for instance, someone hit Nathan. The good part is it has strengthened our relationship, because we are able to see each other so much more.

Having my dad learn the game a little bit after I did was a bit frustrating. Beating his father is every kid's dream. I thought I had won, but last year my dad was playing more hockey than I was, and he almost managed to catch up. That battle is still going on, but it is evident to both of us that I am going to win without breaking a sweat. It's only a matter of time, right?

My father asked me what I expect from hockey for the rest of my life. Earlier today, my dad, my friend Ben and I were playing shinny at Ramsden Park. Everyone else was between thirty and seventy-five, and as I got on the ice I thought it was going to be a cakewalk. I was wrong. On my first shift out I got schooled by someone at least six times my age. I thought to myself that if I can play like that when I am sixty, my life will be worthwhile.

Every kid has dreams, and for a long time mine was to play in the NHL, but watching those guys skate today, I realized there is a lot of great hockey that isn't even close to the big leagues. There are only a few differences between the two games anyway, besides the publicity. One is, in the NHL, if you knock a guy down, you laugh at him. When you're playing for fun, you help him up and you keep playing. The other difference is a million-dollar paycheque.

That part wouldn't be so bad, but I can live without it.

Wesley Allen
March 2005

Catherine Bolt

**LEASIDE PEEWEE SELECT FATHER/SON GAME, APRIL 2005**
*Kneeling, left to right:* Peter Clark, Scott Killien-Clark, Devin
Montrose, Charlie Casper (barely visible behind hair and
crowd), James Bolt (holding cup), Douglas Anderson, Ben
Sankey, Neil Anderson.
*Second Row:* Derek Perry, Jonathan Hart, David Cowie, Brady
DeSantis, Taylor Martin, Alex Small, Wesley Allen, Peter
Holland, Nathan Robbins-Kanter, Aidan Totten, Chris Fallis
(standing, holding stick), Devlin Brand.
*Third Row:* Mike Montrose, Calder Fallis-Naylor, Scott (200 lbs.
of trouble) Cowie, Brad Martin.
*Last Row:* Andrew Bolt, John Sankey (hands on head), Bob
Casper, Terry Fallis, me, Sean Hart, Guy Perry, Tim Fallis,
Roman Kowalczyszyn, Larry Small.

## POSTSCRIPT
### 2004–2005

* Dave Picton moved up to coach the Leaside "A" team. He and the other coaches held tryouts in late May. Wesley showed well at all five tryouts, but they were looking for a defenceman. He was named an alternate.

* Roman took over as head coach of the Leaside Flames pee wee select team. Larry, Alex's father, is the assistant, and although I thought my coaching career should probably have ended by now, I stayed on, too.

* Shawn is now focused on competitive swimming and trains four times per week. He recently broke the central regional time standard for the fifty-metre

freestyle event, beating his previous personal best by more than a second.

- The Vultures continued at New Centre Ice in the summer of 2004. We lost a few players and picked up a few others. Steve became the new goalie. He's very good. After a couple of lopsided wins we were promoted to the "C" division. The Toronto Ice Hockey League, however, didn't make it to the playoffs. It went out of business amid rumours of a buyout by the rink's new manager, Canlan Ice Sports. Canlan advertises itself as "the largest private-sector owner and operator of recreational ice sports facilities in the world." Canlan assumed the rest of our season, but things were messy for a while. They closed one of the rinks at New Centre Ice, and more than once we were playing in so much fog it was hard to see the puck. Still, on a Wednesday night early in September, the Vultures surprised everyone, including ourselves, by winning the championship. Our prize was a box of grey Canlan sweatshirts. I still have mine, although it shrunk in the wash and the sleeves come up to my forearms.

- Five days later, our winter season started at a newer, bigger and better-maintained rink owned by Canlan in Scarborough. It feels like a hockey Wal-Mart, and the restaurant, encased in glass between the complex's four rinks, is loud and has dozens of TVs blaring all the time. There are no stands by the rinks—spectators watch from the restaurant. We lost our first nine games, and in the process dropped from the "C" league to "Rec 2," the lowest one available.

- On September 15, the NHL locked out its players at what would have been the start of the season. The issue was money.

- One of the changes that arrived with the new select season was a rule banning the traditional line of handshakes after the game. Now both teams stay on their respective benches until the referee ensures the dressing-room doors are open. On the ref's signal, the visiting team leaves the ice. When the visiting players are all in their room, the home team goes off. There are severe penalties if the coaches or players break from this routine. The system is an attempt to cut down on postgame brawls.

- Just before Christmas, in a Vancouver court, Todd Bertuzzi pled guilty to charges of assault for his on-ice attack of Steve Moore. B.C. Provincial Court Judge Herb Weitzel gave Bertuzzi a conditional discharge with one year of probation and eighty hours of community service. He will have no criminal record. Bertuzzi is barred from playing hockey during his probation if Steve Moore is on the ice. Moore has shown no intention of returning to hockey.

- Two weeks later, an Edmonton court sentenced Johnathan Way, a twenty-six-year-old defenceman in a local recreational hockey league, to ninety days in jail for his on-ice assault of forty-two-year-old Steve Rae. Way's team, Can Brew, was down by four goals to Rae's team, the Buzzards, with five minutes left in the game. Rae was skating away when Way punched him in the back of the head so hard that Rae dropped to the ice, after which Way punched him again. Rae suffered a concussion, a broken jaw, whiplash and a sprained neck. The attacker maintained he had done nothing wrong.

- In a game with the select team in January, Derek suffered a mild concussion. It was a clean check, but Derek had his head down and the player who hit him was a foot taller and outweighed him by more than twenty pounds.

- Two weeks later, at the select team's return to the Niagara Falls tournament, Wesley's friend Ben was also concussed. I am six feet tall and weigh 185 pounds. The player who hit him was bigger than I am.

- After playing to a tie twice again this season, the Leaside select team met Don Mills for a third time in early February and won after scoring two goals in the final thirty seconds. The last goal went in with two seconds on the clock. The teams have now met eight times in two seasons with four ties, three victories for Don Mills and one for Leaside.

- On February 16, commissioner Gary Bettman announced the official cancellation of the NHL season. The next day's *Globe and Mail* ran a front-page article by Roy MacGregor citing the shinny hockey, road hockey and pond hockey games that are played almost continuously by men and women all across the country, and concluded that "the death of the NHL season has not had the slightest effect on any of it."

- The next day, Steve Moore filed a civil lawsuit against Todd Bertuzzi for civil conspiracy, assault, battery and negligence. Also named in the suit were Canucks forward Brad May, coach Marc Crawford, former general manager Brian Burke, and the partnership that owns the team.

- Late in February, on a Saturday afternoon, Wesley organized a shinny game with Nathan, Ben and Derek at Withrow Park. He collected his skates, gloves and stick and said, "I'm going to play hockey, Dad." All I had to do was say "Have fun," hold the door and watch him go.

- In early March, the select team faced Victoria Village in a best-of-three playoff series. They won the first game 3–0. Winning the second game would give them a free week until the next round, and allow families to enjoy March break without the worry of missing a hockey game. But the second game was a disaster. The referees kept Leaside players in the penalty box for most of the second period, including five full minutes during which Victoria Village held a two-man advantage. The game was tied with two minutes to go when Victoria Village was awarded a penalty shot and won. The third game of the series was in the middle of March break. Wesley was on holiday with me. Leaside lost 1–0.

- Two weeks later Victoria Village eliminated Don Mills from the playoffs, as well. The schoolyard rivalry continues.

- The Vultures were eliminated in the first round of the playoffs in April. Our record for the year at Canlan's Scarborough rink was six wins, seventeen losses and one tie. The Canlan website credited me with two assists and five goals for the season, but I only counted three goals. The summer season starts in May. We're going back to New Centre Ice.

- The same weekend, Wesley played a house-league semifinal playoff game in which he scored six goals and two assists, more in one game than I had managed in the entire season, even if you count the two I didn't really score.

The next week, Wesley's team played for the house-league championship. The game was tied with two minutes to play in the third period when Nathan crossed the blue line on right wing with Wesley trailing at centre. Nathan stayed wide, and when the right defenceman moved to stop him, he passed to Wesley, now alone in front. Wesley scored. They won.

## ABOUT THE AUTHOR

TOM ALLEN is the host of CBC Radio Two's morning show, "Music and Company." He is the author of *Toe Rubber Blues: Mid-Life Thoughts on the Prospects of Aging* and *Rolling Home: A Cross-Canada Railroad Memoir*. Allen lives in Toronto with his two children.